ECHOES OF AN ANGEL

the miraculous **TRUE STORY**
of a boy who lost his eyes but could still see

Echoes of an Angel

AQUANETTA GORDON

WITH CHRIS MACIAS

TYNDALE™
MOMENTUM

An Imprint of
Tyndale House Publishers, Inc.

Published in association with the literary agency of Folio Literary Management, The Film Center Building, 630 Ninth Avenue, Suite 1101, New York, NY 10036.

Library of Congress Cataloging-in-Publication Data

Gordon, Aquanetta.
    Echoes of an angel : the miraculous true story of a boy who lost his eyes but could still see / Aquanetta Gordon, with Chris Macias.
        pages cm
    ISBN 978-1-4143-8622-5 (sc)
1. Underwood, Ben, 1992-2009. 2. Christian children—California—Biography. 3. Blind children—California—Religious life. 4. Echolocation (Physiology) 5. Cancer patients—Religious life. I. Title.
    BR1715.U53G67 2014
    277.3'083092—dc23
    [B]   2013049779

Printed in the United States of America

20   19   18   17   16   15   14
 7   6   5   4   3   2   1

I DEDICATE THIS BOOK TO MY CHILDREN:

Joe Johnson, Derius Johnson, Tiffany Johnson,
Ben Underwood, and Isaiah Bridgett.
I thank God for each of you, and I'm so blessed to be your mother.

"We have to, right now, pull our united family together so that we can celebrate the goodness that Ben talked about in his life and that God has promised us all since the very beginning. The God that we serve does say, 'Impossible is unacceptable.'"

STEVIE WONDER, SPEAKING AT BEN UNDERWOOD'S MEMORIAL SERVICE ON JANUARY 26, 2009

CONTENTS

INTRODUCTION

JANUARY 1995

My first thought as I walked into the surgical recovery room was how small my baby looked. I'd probably paced back and forth a thousand miles in hospital waiting rooms. I'd tended to surgery scars so fresh they made me wince. But nothing could have prepared me for this.

Ben, who was not quite three, was still groggy, and bandages covered everything above his nose. The brightly lit room was filled with other patients recovering from operations, and the sounds of machines monitoring everyone's vital signs ping-ponged around me. Ben was hooked up to IVs, his lips parted and slightly chapped. His body was dwarfed by the machines monitoring his breathing and heart rate. Once I was at his bedside, I placed my hand on Ben's arm to let him know that I was there and that I loved him. He was just so young and so little—and now he would have to learn to live without his eyes. I wanted to be the first person Ben touched when he finally awoke.

As I stroked his hand, Ben mustered enough energy to speak. What he said made my heart shatter.

"Mom, I can't see anymore!" he said, his voice a strained whisper. "What's wrong with my eyes? I can't see anymore!"

It took every ounce of strength to fight back my tears. I knelt over Ben and put his little hands on my face.

"Yes, you can see, baby!" I struggled to speak in my happiest voice. "You can see me with your hands!"

I felt Ben's fingers wriggle over my face. Then I brought my face close to him.

"You smell me?" I asked him. "That means you can see me with your nose. That's a way of seeing me too!"

I gently tugged his tiny ear.

"Hear me? That means you can see me with your ears."

I took a deep breath and hugged him as closely as I could.

"Baby, you don't have eyes anymore—but you can see me with your ears, you can see me with your nose, and you can see me with your hands. That means you can still see me!"

My boy may have lost his eyesight that day, but I was going to be sure he never thought of himself as blind. And as I later discovered, Ben could see—just differently from you and me.

■ ■ ■

SUMMER 2013

As I let my eyelids close, the memory makes me smile. It always does.

My mind drifts back to a summer evening in our south Sacramento neighborhood. I feel the cool breeze tickling my skin and catch a few whiffs of barbecue smoke teasing my nose. A group of kids ride their beat-up bikes around our cul-de-sac of tract homes. I hear laughter and yelling as they pedal faster and faster.

They've set up a little wooden ramp in the middle of the street. One by one they circle around, launching themselves into the air over and over again, scraped shins and all. They've been at it for a good hour now: white kids, Mexican kids, a couple of Vietnamese kids from down the block—and a seven-year-old black kid in an oversize yellow T-shirt and baggy jeans.

That's Ben. And he's the fastest of them all.

"Hey, y'all!" Ben yells to the others. "Get out of my way!"

I watch Ben pump his bike pedals furiously, picking up speed as he turns toward the ramp. As long as Ben makes his sound, I know he'll be okay.

The closer Ben gets to the ramp, the faster he clicks with his tongue. In his mind, the ramp begins to take shape:

Click

Click click

Click click click

Clickclickclickclickclick

He rolls straight into the middle of the ramp, pulls his bike into a wheelie, and flies into the air. It's only a second of flight, but I know he loves it. It's one of those moments of freedom that kids live for. He'd do this all day if it were up to him.

"Ben!" I yell. "Will you come put that bike away and get in the house already? You know it's your turn to set the table tonight." No response. "Ben! Are you listening to me?"

"Mom, hold up!" he yells back, skidding his rear tire. "I'm just going to jump one more time."

"Boy, you better hurry up!"

I open my eyes and smile.

■ ■ ■

Because of Ben, I now know that there's such a thing as vision beyond sight. True vision doesn't come from the eyes but from the soul. I learned from Ben that even if you are blind, faith will guide you in ways you never thought possible. That life has no limits, no matter what physical, mental, or emotional challenges come your way.

That blindness is only a state of mind.

CHAPTER 1

COUNTRY GIRL

THE OUTSKIRTS OF BLYTHE, CALIFORNIA: MID-1960S

Ben found freedom flying over ramps on his bike; at age seven, I found freedom exploring the California desert on foot. On most of the long, hot summer days, my brothers, younger sister, and I headed out to an irrigation canal, fed by the lower Colorado River, in one of the farm fields near our home.

Often we'd grab our fishing poles from the back of the house first. That way, after spending hours swimming, we could dry out as we dangled our feet over the edge of a canal and cast out our fishing lines. When we got hungry at noontime, we'd race home for peanut butter and jelly sandwiches. A few minutes later, we'd slam the screen door behind us as we ran back outside.

If you've ever heard the term "living in the sticks" or "in the boonies," you have a good idea of what Blythe was like. It's in the Sonoran Desert near the California-Arizona border. That's about a three-hours' drive from San Bernardino and Riverside.

I loved growing up in Blythe. I never stayed in the house playing with dolls. I was a little tomboy who liked to be out playing with sticks, jumping off stuff, and swimming in the canals that watered the thousands of acres of corn, alfalfa, and melons that grew in southeastern California.

The air outside smelled so fresh and unpolluted, and with the next house a quarter mile down the road, we had all the space we'd ever want. To me, this was rich living. There was always something to do—like hitchhiking into downtown Blythe, nine miles away; riding on our neighbor's donkey; or playing with the pigs my daddy raised for our family. Sometimes I'd ride them around the pigpen, holding on to their ears as they cried, *Squeeeee! Squeeeee!*

In the summertime, though, we always seemed to end up swimming in one of those irrigation ditches. It was so hot! I remember the temperature once hitting 120 degrees. Back then, kids played outside all day, returning home to stay only at nightfall, when the endless blue skies gave way to the pitch-black of night.

Even in the middle of nowhere, I had plenty of playmates. I have four brothers and two sisters, and I'm right in the middle. We were surrounded by lots of extended family too. My grandmother raised thirteen kids, which meant I had about two dozen cousins and other relatives to play with. Though we didn't have much money, we didn't ask for much either. Our life was simple but happy.

We'd sometimes get in a little mischief, as kids do. Some of us would steal bottles from a local factory and sell them back for pocket money. Another time, a few other kids and I went door-to-door saying we were raising money for disabled kids—but we kept the money for ourselves. I didn't think we were doing any harm, but looking back now, I should've known better. When I had my own kids, I sure didn't let them think that kind of thing was okay.

My childhood was the best of times, even with our family of nine crowded into a shack. And yes, it was truly a shack—a wooden house that was barely holding up, old and musty-smelling on the inside. We had three bedrooms, a small living room, and a cramped kitchen that led straight to the back door. Wild cats skittered around the property, and once in a while a snake would find its way inside the house. That's how country we were, and it was all part of the adventure.

A lot of people ask me about my name, Aquanetta. I was named after Acquanetta Ross, a Native American actress from the 1940s. She was nicknamed "the Venezuelan Volcano" and featured in a bunch of silly movies like *Tarzan and the Leopard Woman*. Acquanetta and her husband later owned a car dealership in Arizona, and she appeared in their commercials. I believe my mother liked the name because it sounded unique. My family calls me "Aq" for short.

My dad was about twenty years older than my mom. When Mom and Dad met, she already had two kids and was pregnant with one of my brothers. I was their first child together, and they'd go on to have three more. I was actually born in the car on the way to the hospital in Riverside. My birth certificate lists my birthplace as "Highway 99, three miles east of Indio."

My father, Ben Gordon, was my hero as a kid. He was a tall, strong man, about six feet three with a medium-dark complexion. He loved his children, and I thought he was the best dad in the world. He was a sweet guy, and all the women fawned over him. Everybody, in fact, respected him so much that they'd say, "Don't mess with Big Gordon's kids!"

My dad worked as an agriculturalist, driving tractors and irrigating fields for a living. Sometimes we'd go to work with him and ride on the tractors, then come home dirty and happy. He'd even let us take our own lap around the fields on the tractor.

My dad rarely laid an angry hand on us. One time when I was playing with my siblings in a field near our house, we thought it would be fun to light and throw matches and then see how quickly we could stomp out the flames. Well, we weren't as quick putting them out as we'd hoped. One of the matches started a fire, and the flames got too big for us to control. We started yelling, and my dad ran over to put out the fire. Oh, he was mad.

"What are you kids trying to do?" he yelled. "Are you trying to burn down Blythe or something?"

We all got a whupping for that one. That was the first time Dad ever spanked me. It didn't hurt, but I screamed like he was trying to kill me.

What I remember most about my dad is his kindness. He'd pick up hitchhikers. He'd give money to people even though he didn't have much of his own. He was a man with a lot of love to give, and we all felt lucky to be around him. He didn't play favorites with any of us. If there were seven kids in the house and he came home with five extra dollars, nobody got any. He wouldn't give out spending money unless he had enough for everyone.

I didn't get along with my mom very well. I grew up feeling like she hated me. Her father had picked and chosen favorites among his own kids. If he loved you, he really loved you. And if he didn't like you, it was almost as if you weren't one of his kids. My mom treated her kids the same way. My sister Denise and I were a year apart, but Denise could get anything and go anywhere she wanted.

Nothing I did seemed to make my mom happy. I remember cowering between our stove and the wall once, trying to get away from her because she was beating me with a leather belt. The crazy thing? She was angry because my sister wasn't folding clothes with me. For some reason, she took it out on me. My grandmother stepped in that time and forced my mom to stop.

As a young girl, I tried so hard to satisfy my mother. I studied a lot so I could make straight As. I played sports, and I ran so fast that I should've run in the Olympics. But not once did I ever hear her say, "I'm proud of you."

My parents had a fairly good relationship, until they'd drink and start fighting. Then, boy, would they have some really nasty moments. My mom ran over my dad one time while we were packed in the family car. They'd been arguing about something—I was too little to understand what had triggered that fight—but it got heated as we pulled into a gas station. When my dad got out to pay for the gas, my mom jumped into the driver's seat and hit the accelerator. She smashed into my dad and pinned him against a wall. Both of his legs were broken, and the doctors told him he might never walk again. He did walk, although from then on he had a limp.

My dad had to face a bigger health challenge when I was about eight years old. That's when he was diagnosed with colon cancer. I still remember the two men in suits who came all the way from Riverside to our house in Blythe to deliver the test results to my dad. I listened to them talk to him. I didn't know what cancer was, but it sounded scary. I started screaming and hollering, and my dad had to throw me out of the room. Soon afterward, he began a long journey of battling cancer and enduring many hardships that would last the rest of his life.

■ ■ ■

My parents separated when I was in fifth grade. My dad stayed in Blythe, and the rest of us moved to a beat-up house on the east side of Riverside, nearly 175 miles to the west. The simple, carefree life I loved was no more.

I really missed my dad. One time I ran away from home and caught the Greyhound bus to Blythe to be with him. When I showed up, I told my dad that my mom had sent me. Sometimes I'd pray and ask God for my dad to come pick me up and take me home with him. If he didn't show up right then, he'd pull up the next day in his white pickup truck. That's how I knew the Lord was hearing my prayers.

At least, that's what it seemed like to a little girl who felt loved by her father and rejected by her mother. If I wanted to see my dad, I'd pray, and then I'd see him. The same thing seemed to happen when it rained. If I prayed for it to stop, it stopped. As a girl, prayer seemed like magic to me.

During this time, my dad continued his battle with colon cancer. He'd undergone one chemotherapy treatment, but it made him sick, so he wouldn't do it again. He tried his best to carry on with his life, and he continued to work and handle his business. He never complained even once. If he was feeling bad at any point, he sure didn't show it.

By the time I was eleven, I had taken on a lot of responsibilities. Once again, I just wanted to make my mom happy. I'd get up around three or four in the morning and hear her say, "Aq, I know you're up!" Then she'd let me know what she needed me to do that day. Usually I'd help my little brother Ernest throw newspapers on his paper route and then I'd come home and help some of my other siblings get ready for the day. I'd fix them something to eat and walk them to school.

I'd also help my mom handle her finances by writing checks and paying bills for her. My older sister, Diane, became a mom at fifteen, and I'd sometimes take care of my niece and nephew. I did everything, but it was fun. I had the energy to do it, and I never got tired. I think I'm hyperactive. To this day, I can still go and go on just a few hours of sleep.

As busy as I was at home, I managed to earn straight As. I was very outgoing and always wanted to help people. I remember one girl in my class who always came to school looking dirty. She'd have spit caked in the corners of her mouth, and she wore dirty pants with holes in them. That made her an easy target for kids who wanted someone to pick on.

One day a boy kicked her books over. I didn't like to see people picking on others, so I stepped in and said, "You better leave her alone! Who do you think you are?"

Pretty soon I started beating up that boy and gave him a bloody nose. Our teacher broke up the fight and sent him straight to the principal's office. The teacher said I had to go to the office too. He didn't want to send me, but he had to because he saw the whole thing.

Getting in trouble was new to me. But I'm glad I stuck up for that poor girl and taught that bully a lesson. Looking back now, I see why the Lord gave me a feisty spirit. I'd need to tap into that as an adult when my son Ben had to deal with his own school issues.

My grandparents had moved from Blythe to Riverside several years before we did. Now we lived just a few houses down from them. Although my grandfather was mean like my mom, my grandmother was one of the most giving people I've ever known. She sowed a lot of love, and poor as she was, she always seemed to have enough to give away. I never saw her turn anyone away from her table.

We weren't a churchgoing family in those days. Since my grandparents didn't grow up in church, I guess that's understandable. But when I was about twelve years old, my sister Denise and I went to a summer youth program at a local university. One day the counselor who led my sister's group, a lady named Andrea Jones, invited us to Riverside Faith Temple. I started going to the church every Tuesday night, to Bible study on Friday night, and to services on Sunday morning and Sunday night. A church bus would pick me up. Man, that church was an awesome place!

As you can probably tell by now, I've always been competitive, and I want to come in first in anything I try. Well, the church had group competitions to encourage students to memorize Bible passages. That's how I learned many of the Scriptures that never left me, even in my darkest times. I always loved Psalm 23 and that sense of the Lord as my shepherd, guiding me. I also memorized the Beatitudes from Matthew 5:

> Blessed are the poor in spirit,
>   For theirs is the kingdom of heaven.
> Blessed are those who mourn,
>   For they shall be comforted.
> Blessed are the meek,
>   For they shall inherit the earth. (verses 3-5, NKJV)

I'm so grateful to Andrea Jones for inviting me to Riverside Faith Temple. By the time I was fourteen, I knew how it felt to be loved and held close by God. I didn't know all the stories and teaching in the Bible yet, and I still had a long way to go in my faith journey, but I believed that God was real. Whenever I prayed, I knew He was right there listening. For me, going to the Lord in prayer would be a refuge throughout my life, even when I made poor choices and strayed from God's path. There would be times when I felt far from Him because of what I'd done, but He was never far from me.

■■■

My dad's health started to slip in the summer of 1976, about five years after his original diagnosis. He could no longer get out of bed and had trouble controlling his bowels. Even so, he still found joy in the little pleasures of life. When he was able, he made us kids our favorite iced tea with lemon. It was so good! He'd find ways to give us spending money. That's the kind of man he was.

I was by my dad's side on his deathbed. His last wish was to see all of his kids one final time. It was hard to see my strong dad so frail and suffering so much, but he didn't complain. We gathered around as he asked us to feed him cool chunks of watermelon. He died that same day. He was sixty-eight years old. I was fourteen.

Losing my dad was devastating. We were all close to him, but I always felt like I was special to my dad. After he died, I became terrified that I'd get cancer too. If I got a little bump or a knot on my wrist, I'd think, *Oh no, I've got cancer!*

I'll always carry the grief of losing my dad at such a young age, but I did my best to keep going strong, just like he wanted me to. During eighth grade at my junior high in Riverside, I was straight As all the way, and physically strong too. There wasn't a boy who could beat me in track, kickball—absolutely anything.

I was a star student that year, but when I graduated, the school gave the honor roll award to a popular white girl. I'd run for class secretary and didn't get it, even though I knew I'd gotten the most votes. That broke my spirit. I mean, it just broke me. Part of me didn't even want to care anymore.

I'd always been a go-getter kind of girl, but I couldn't help feeling alone and like all my hard work didn't matter. I had too much pride to let my grades drop, but I no longer gave my all at school. I remember watching a girl run track one spring day, knowing inside that I could run circles around her but not even caring enough to try.

I wasn't angry—just discouraged. I wanted to achieve, to break through the dysfunction in my family, but I had no one to show me how. I'd have to figure out life on my own, relying on trial and plenty of error. But in the meantime, I was sixteen, and like a lot of teen girls, I was suddenly interested in boys. I let go of a lot of dreams and a desire to better myself. I even stopped going to Riverside Faith Temple.

It would be easy to look back and cry about what could have been. Instead, when I got older, I channeled my hurt into the determination that no one would ever discriminate against my kids or tell them what they couldn't do. I would back up my own kids 100 percent and always be willing to fight for them.

CHAPTER 2

HITTING BOTTOM

I LEFT HOME at seventeen after asking a simple question.

My younger sister and her boyfriend had moved to New York with their young child. My mother became their sole source of finances; I simply asked my mom why she was sending them money. Instead of answering me, she began hitting me, even as she kept driving. That was it. I'd finally had enough. I jumped out of that moving car and never returned home. It would be five years before I even spoke to my mom again.

At first, I stayed with my grandmother. By this time, all of her kids were grown except my aunt Cynthia, who was the baby girl of her thirteen children. Cynthia and I were the same age and went to the same school, so it was like moving in with a sister. Our high school graduation was just a few months away when I went to live with her and my grandmother.

When I was eighteen, I started dating Joe, who later became the father of my first three children. He was about eight years older than I was. We had our first child together, Joe James Johnson Jr., about a year later.

Those years were hard. I was a young mother who'd left home and was now trying to find my purpose in the world. I believe in my heart that I wanted to have a baby because I was looking for love, and I knew I could find that in a child. That wasn't the right motivation. It's just that, in my upbringing, we weren't taught how to have a healthy relationship or a solid family life. But I did know how to take care of children.

I wouldn't trade my son for anything, but looking back, I wish I had known how to make wiser choices. I still believed in God, but I was young in my faith at that time and didn't understand that the way I was living wasn't what He wanted for me. It would be many years, and many mistakes, before I learned how to follow God's plan for my life. In the meantime, I mostly figured I was on my own to do the best I could.

My relationship with Joe seemed good at first. He was a working man, and I moved into his apartment. We never married, but that wasn't unusual in my family, where the attitude was, *Don't bother getting married, or you'll just have the hassle of a divorce later on.*

When Joe's company closed down, we had to move in with his mother. I didn't want to be a burden on someone, but we didn't have any other options. We eventually got our own apartment through Section 8, a government housing program. These were modest, low-income units near Riverside, in an area you'd call "the hood."

My life took a very sad and dangerous detour when I was introduced to crack cocaine. I'll never forget that day I first tried it. I was at my uncle's house with a couple of other family members. Several of us sat around, smoking it.

Once I tried that drug, it immediately became a part of my life. I was addicted and began using it regularly. I had no idea how easily I could become dependent on that evil stuff. I guess I was looking for an escape, a feeling of ultimate happiness after all the hard times and poverty I'd experienced. But instead of making me happy, crack turned my life completely upside down.

I stopped using drugs when I found out I was pregnant with my second child, Derius. Thank God he was fine when he was born. But the pull of that sinister smoke drove me back into a life of sin; I started using again after Derius was born. Then I got pregnant with my daughter, Tiffany. I had babies nearly back-to-back, and again I stopped using drugs once I knew I was pregnant. Everything was fine with Tiffany when she was born, but those drugs still had me hooked. My world was starting to collapse around me.

Any hope I had of building a future with Joe disappeared when I discovered he'd cheated on me. He was a decent guy at heart, but that hadn't stopped him from cheating, and the betrayal took its toll. I said, "I'm done with this." I decided I'd rather live on the street than in that madness, so that's what I prepared to do. I let Joe keep our older son since he was about four years old and would be starting school soon.

I was about to become homeless, and Joe-Joe needed more stability than I could give him.

My possessions didn't matter so much. I was once a contestant on *The Price Is Right*, where I won furniture and a bunch of other stuff. I left all that in our apartment and decided that sleeping in my car was a better option. I was determined to make a new life, even if that meant starting from scratch.

With so many relatives nearby, we always had a place to hang out during the day. But at night I parked my little red Chevette around the corner from my grandma's house and slept inside of it. I'd lie in the backseat with a blanket and pillow to keep Derius and me warm. I was actually pregnant with my daughter, Tiffany, during this time.

Cynthia would come down the street and cry, "Aqua, you don't have to be out here in this car! Please come up here to the house!"

But I was stubborn. "No, Cynthia. I'm okay. Don't worry about me. I'll make it."

I didn't know what I was going to do, but I just couldn't be in that apartment with Joe. I actually had a lot of peace of mind. This was my mess, and I wasn't blaming anyone or looking for a handout. I'd made my bed, and now I had to lie in it—even if that bed was the backseat of a tiny red hatchback.

The demons of drug addiction made it hard to move forward. During all the time that I used drugs, I hated it. I hated myself for doing them, especially as my health suffered. I'd always been thin, but now I got really skinny.

As much as I despised what the drugs were doing to me, I felt drawn to spend time with those friends who were in the drug scene too. Yet it got to the point that my stomach would hurt when I'd see them because I knew what we were going to do together. In some strange way, I knew that the person puffing from a crack pipe was not really me! My addiction was like a sickness, but no matter how pitiful I felt, that evil craving got the best of me. I lived to experience the rush. But it wouldn't last long, and then I'd want to do it again.

Drugs are tools of Satan that rob us of so much goodness in our lives—our families, health, and happiness. When we use drugs, they cloud our vision and put distance between us and God.

■ ■ ■

I thank God that I could count on at least some of my family to have my back. My grandmother, Cynthia, and other relatives helped make sure my family got what they needed. I cringe in thinking how my life might've gone without that help. I never had to worry about us going hungry. There was always something to eat, and my babies had diapers. I didn't have much stability in my life, but the Lord blessed me with some wonderful family.

I still didn't have my own home when Tiffany was born, but a friend of the family who lived near Long Beach took us in. Yet the drama didn't stop. Joe's new woman, who'd been my babysitter, reported to Child Protective Services (CPS) that I was on drugs. About a month later, they took Tiffany.

Then they took Derius. My son Joe stayed with his father. I was truly left with nothing.

Later, one of my aunts got custody of my kids, but she let me take care of them. Even with my kids back, though, I couldn't shake my addictions. I'd hit rock bottom as a mom. By this time, Tiffany was about six months old and Derius was a year and a half—still just babies.

After a while, another family member called CPS, telling them I wasn't supposed to have my kids. I was still living in Long Beach with friends. They had a fairly luxurious home at a fashionable address. When the police came to take my babies, they looked around at my kids, who were obviously well cared for, and asked, "Why are we here? Why are we taking these kids?"

The social worker who showed up with the police quickly explained the situation—from her viewpoint. She seemed angry that I had my children and stomped around the room before practically grabbing my kids, who looked terrified, and pulling them away from me. Knowing I could do nothing to prevent CPS from taking them was awful and scary. I felt as if the social worker simply enjoyed showing she had power over me and there was nothing I could do about it. Her ugly sneer reinforced the message that I was getting no sympathy from her.

Soon after Derius and Tiffany were placed in foster care, I learned that they had been put in separate homes. At the very least, I wanted my son and daughter to be together. I wasn't told which families had them, or even whether they were with African American families.

I got one hour two times a month with Tiffany and Derius, in a room with someone watching over us. Thinking back to the first visit makes me want to cry. I walked into the small room, which didn't have much more than a table and a few chairs. My heart broke as I looked at Derius and Tiffany, who were sitting next to the social worker.

I had the feeling that my children, especially Derius, weren't being looked after properly. The family who were fostering him didn't want to deal with his long hair, so they'd cut it short. My kids had never been sick, even when we were living in a car, but during our visit I could tell that Derius had a bad cold. He'd also stopped talking the way he used to. Derius had regressed to simply mimicking the last few words that I'd say.

"My baby's not talking anymore!" I said to the social worker.

"Oh, he doesn't know who you are," she answered.

"Yes, he does know who I am," I shot back. "I am his mother!"

The social worker rolled her eyes and ignored me.

I know she was just doing her job, but her attitude ripped me up inside. I loved my children, and watching this social worker take them away and treat me like I wasn't worthy of being a parent was almost more than I could stand.

The worst way to hurt a mother is to take her children. It hurt so much hearing Derius and Tiffany cry for me when my time was up—almost as if a knife were cutting through my heart. I felt like I'd failed them. Much of this was my fault, especially because of my drug addiction, but that

CHAPTER 3

GOD'S PLAN

I GOT A JOB packing cups in a factory. I found a two-bedroom house that was so tiny you could pivot on one foot and touch everything in the kitchen, but it was a home.

Thank God, he had a plan for me. Through all the hardship and the turmoil I'd gone through, the Lord never let me fall completely. It was around this time that I started going back to Riverside Faith Temple. Between the ages of twelve and sixteen, I'd been in church practically every time the doors were open. I'd always felt that God's hands were on me. But in the years since, I'd backslid into all this worldly stuff. I wanted to get back to that place where I felt so safe and protected in God's presence. Sometimes I'd break into prayer and plead with the Lord for forgiveness, drawing on some bits of Bible passages, especially Psalm 51:

Jesus, you are awesome. I appreciate your goodness, your love, and your mercy. I pray for more mercy, God, for I am a mess.

Jesus, you are so wonderful. No matter all my messes, I love you and know that you have loved me first.

Please, O Lord, keep me humble. I pray to be used by you, O Lord. My sole desire is to do your perfect will, to work and build your Kingdom.

Have mercy upon me according to your loving-kindness. According to the multitude of your tender mercies, blot out my transgressions. Cleanse me, Lord, from my sin; wash me, and I shall be whiter than snow.

I went to Riverside Faith Temple to bring in the new year of 1989. I'll never forget that night because I was feeling so heartbroken about not having custody of my children.

I was sitting by myself in the front row of the church, all the way to the right. The choir started to sing "Thank You, Lord," and everybody joined in worship and praise. In the midst of those beautiful voices, sobs started to well up inside me. All of the heaviness I'd been going through—battling drugs, losing my kids, missing my father so much even though he'd been gone many years by then—weighed down my soul and left me wounded. I desperately needed salvation.

I closed my eyes tightly, feeling my face grow wet with tears. Then Pastor Joseph Sims came up and touched my hands. He spoke to me, gently and firmly: "Aqua, there's this glow all around you. Jesus loves you and accepts you. Your life has been blessed, and you will forever be safe with him."

I kept crying even as he told me all this, because I felt the

Lord was holding me and soothing all of my pain and hurts. I feel like crying now just remembering that night.

God held me close, and he never let go. At every step along the way, he reminded me, "I will never leave you nor forsake you" (Hebrews 13:5). And even in my lowest moments, through all my hardships, he was still there.

Then he did something amazing. It didn't seem all that miraculous at the time, but it changed me and my family forever. After about two months with Child Protective Services, Derius and Tiffany were placed with a Christian family: Pastor Lewis Pugh and his wife, Devon, from New Creation Christian Church in Moreno Valley. They had four children of their own—twin daughters, a son, and a baby daughter—and also ran their own day care. The Pughs loved children and were interested in adopting.

I couldn't help feeling skeptical and hurt when I first met Devon. She called to set up a time for us to meet and for me to visit with my children. We agreed to get together at a park near her home. As kind as Devon sounded when she called, I was furious with this unfamiliar voice on the line because I was sure she was trying to take my place.

My heart grew colder and colder as I walked up to Devon for the first time in that park. My guard was up so high that it might as well have been a fortress. Who was this woman pretending to be my children's mother? I knew that no other person was going to love my kids like me, their true mother. The Pughs had my children, and the idea that some people viewed me as an unfit parent had filled me with tremendous bitterness.

Once Devon introduced herself, I was so mad, I could barely speak. I just nodded quietly while she told me I'd get to visit my kids for two hours each week. In spite of the way I acted, Devon didn't sink to my level. She was so sweet and did her best to try to calm me down.

The Pughs ministered to me so kindly and patiently that over time I realized they were there to help me and my family, not to try and bump me out of my babies' lives. That's what the love of God can do: it can take all the bitterness in the world and melt it away. Though she wasn't much older than me, Devon became like a second mother to me. That realization hit me hard the day I stopped at the home of my mother, whom everyone called Pat, on my way to visit my kids at the Pughs.

"Do you want to come with me to see Derius and Tiffany?" I asked her.

She appeared to have been drinking and simply waved me off. Something inside me broke.

"Pat, why do you hate me?" I asked. "And why did you give Denise anything she wanted?"

She looked at me and gave a slight shrug. "Your sister needed me. You could take care of yourself."

It wasn't a very satisfying answer to a woman like me who'd spent years trying to get her mom's approval. Sadly, that was the deepest conversation my mother and I ever had, and we never got a chance to reconcile. She died before Tiffany turned one.

As painful as that moment was, that's also when I realized that God could show his love for me through people I wasn't even related to. I was comforted by the Pughs treating me like a human being and not like a drug addict who wasn't worthy of her children. In their compassion, they didn't look at my faults—they looked at my heart.

So when Devon invited me to her church, I agreed to go. New Creation Christian Church was a small congregation, made up of just five families. As the Pughs and I prayed together, Devon showed me love like a sister, asking the Lord to help me find healing and a new beginning. In my heart, I prayed that I would get my kids back. I wanted this more than anything, and I pleaded for God to help me.

It wasn't long until I became the praise and worship leader at New Creation. I was happy to help with anything the church leaders wanted me to do. I'm not a good singer, but I'd get up and sing for the Lord. From the people there, I learned so much about how to walk with the Lord and live by his Word. I could say "I love you," but that's just a bunch of words until it's acted out. I had to learn to live the Scripture, not just quote it. Then the love would become alive, like the Word of God. The Pughs taught me how to love—not by telling me, but by showing me.

The foster care authorities wanted Devon to keep Tiffany and Derius for good, and she very much wanted to adopt them. Devon's daughters would carry Tiffany around like a favorite baby doll, and their entire family doted on my kids.

Though adoption papers were already being drafted, giving up my kids wasn't meant to be. The Pughs were always a praying family, and in one moment of reflection, Devon heard the Lord speaking to her heart. The message caught her off guard. She felt the Lord tell her, *You will not adopt these children. You will reconcile these children back to their mother and their mother back to me.*

The next day I called Devon, crying and begging for my babies back. This broke Devon's heart because she'd become so close to my kids and truly wanted to be their new mother. Yet she stayed obedient to the Lord's word and said, "Okay, you will have them back."

Devon wanted to see me succeed and be the mother I was meant to be. She began allowing me to take Derius and Tiffany for extended visits. She let me pick them up on Friday and bring them back on Sunday. Instead of the resentment I'd once felt, I now considered her Sister Devon. My children loved her, I loved her, and I couldn't have hoped for a better person in my life.

I realized how God works out things that the devil intends for evil, so that bitterness can be transformed into sweetness. When I look back, I think of what the Bible says in Romans 8:28: "We know that God causes everything to work together for the good of those who love God and are called according to his purpose for them" (NLT).

That's not to say getting back on track was easy. I had all these aspirations to better myself and straighten out my life by getting more education. I had the idea of working as a court reporter, but I didn't know the process it takes to become one. I never had anyone to take me to a college and show me around.

The good news was that I'd largely beaten back my drug addiction. I'd also quit smoking cigarettes, even though my habit had once gotten so bad that I was going through a pack to a pack and a half a day. I didn't enter any kind of rehabilitation program but was able to find strength through the grace of God. I'd go to church and pray for the Lord to take away my addictions and bad habits. I put my last pack down on a Sunday after church, and it's been more than twenty years since I've touched a cigarette.

Quitting drugs for good was a lot tougher. I'd quit for up to a year at a time, but they'd come sneaking back into my life. Still, I was trying my best to improve myself and earn the right to raise my own children. I enrolled in classes at Riverside Community College and got a job in the jewelry department at Target. I focused as hard as I could, pouring everything I had into the goal of getting my babies back.

Once I started going to church regularly, lots of good things began to happen in my life. The biggest blessing was that I finally regained custody of my kids. Derius and Tiffany had been in foster care for over a year, and I'd taken parenting classes to help get them back. I won custody of Joe Jr. about six months later. We'd all gone through so much turmoil, but now our little family was once again complete and we could start moving forward.

I was beginning to understand how God was directing my life. If I did wrong, I'd get caught. But if I followed him and did the right thing, my circumstances worked out much better. I realized I couldn't continue abusing drugs anymore. That wasn't me. The real me had been hidden away, obscured by clouds of drug smoke. I was meant for better things, especially being a good mother and a proper role model for my kids. I had to change. This transformation wouldn't happen overnight, and I made some bad decisions that would continue to frustrate me and weigh heavily on my conscience. But at least I could better see the guiding light that the Lord had shined down the path for me. He already had a plan, and he was working all those things out, although I didn't recognize the full scope and glory of his will until later.

■ ■ ■

I met Stephen Underwood at my aunt's house on a beautiful spring day in April 1991.

It's kind of a funny story. Steve worked for Southern California Edison doing what I do now: disconnecting people for nonpayment. He came to my aunt's door to tell her he either needed to collect money for the electricity bill or he'd have to turn off the power. My aunt couldn't pay the bill, but I talked Stephen into keeping her power on. I said I'd go on a date with him to sweeten the deal.

Steve swept me right off my feet. It wasn't long before he was cooking for me and romancing me. He would pick me up and carry me in his arms. As a single mom, I enjoyed being pampered for a change. He was so loving and giving that the age difference between us seemed to melt away. I was twenty-nine, and he was forty-four.

Looking back, it's clear that getting involved with Steve was not what God wanted for me—though I'm so thankful the Lord gave me my son Ben. I must have gotten pregnant the first time Steve and I were together, but I didn't think of that possibility at the moment because it seemed so perfect. Yet if I'd looked at it from the outside, it wasn't an ideal situation. Steve had been divorced for only two years, and we didn't know each other that well. He was already the father of two daughters, one in her midtwenties and the other a teenager. But we were in love, and as far as I was concerned, nothing else mattered.

I wasn't sure how Steve would react to the news that he was going to be a father again. When I told him, Steve was initially happy about it. That was a relief, but I still felt like I had to get right with God. I knew he loved me no matter what I did, but I also knew getting pregnant like this wasn't God's plan.

I was so nervous about telling Pastor Pugh and Sister Devon I was pregnant. They are two of God's most beautiful creations and truly know how to love unconditionally, but I felt like I'd let both them and myself down. Still, they never judged me. All they ever wanted was to give me guidance and love.

The truth was that Sister Devon already knew I was pregnant—not from the size of my belly but because the Holy Spirit told her. My jaw just about hit the floor when she asked one night, "Aquanetta, you aren't going to tell me you're with child?"

I broke down and started crying.

"You can't hide things from God," Sister Devon said, trying to console me. "The Holy Spirit tells us everything. It's not to embarrass you or anything. It's to help you and love you."

At that time, I was homeless again after moving my family

out of a bad environment. Now that I was pregnant, I knew I needed to get away from the lure of drugs. For two months, I'd been searching unsuccessfully for a new place to live, so I planned to leave Riverside and move to Sacramento with my brother.

I visited the Pughs one Sunday to tell them good-bye. Sister Devon let me know that the Lord had spoken to her heart that morning and told her to take us in. At first I was uneasy. *These were the foster parents for my kids*, I thought. *Now they're going to foster-parent me, too?*

Yet I knew it was the right thing to do, so we went to stay with them. The morning after we moved in, I applied to lease a two-bedroom duplex, and my application was immediately approved. That was a miracle in itself. We lived with the Pughs for three weeks until the house was ready for us to move into. During the time we lived in their home, the Pughs taught me so much about how to live in the Word. They would get me up in the morning, and we'd all pray together: for continued blessings, for the health of my unborn baby, and more.

Even after the kids and I had moved into our new house, the Pughs kept close tabs on us. They told me that if I needed any kind of help or support, all I had to do was ask. Not long afterward, I called the Pughs at 2 a.m. to tell them I was going into labor. Though I had a lot of extended family in the area, I wanted the Pughs with me at the hospital.

CHAPTER 4

LEARNING TO BE MOM

RIVERSIDE, CALIFORNIA: JANUARY 26, 1992

I held my newborn close to my heart and looked into his wide, brown eyes. Benjamin Alonzo Underwood had come into the world just hours earlier, a beautiful boy weighing six pounds eleven ounces. Snuggled in the hospital bed at Parkview Community Hospital, I stroked his soft head and marveled at his alert little face. Everything about Ben was perfect to me. I thanked the Lord for blessing me with such a beautiful child.

Although I'd had an unusually easy labor, this had been a difficult pregnancy in other ways. For one thing, I could no longer count on Ben's father being in his life, despite his initial excitement about my pregnancy. We would stay in touch for the sake of our baby, but we had drifted apart by the time Ben was born.

Relations between Steve and me had been strained for several months. For one thing, Steve wasn't too happy when I told him I was going back to church. He was a Jehovah's Witness and could be disassociated by his church because I belonged to a different faith. On top of that, we'd had a child out of wedlock. His family members were very devoted Jehovah's Witnesses, and he wasn't even supposed to date anyone outside their faith. Stephen loved his parents and didn't want to disappoint them, so that kept us from developing a truly strong relationship.

Though we both decided it wasn't going to work, it wasn't a bad split. Stephen even wanted our child to be named after him. That wasn't going to happen. My baby was going to be named Ben, in honor of my father, the greatest man I have ever known.

My little family spent ten days with the Pughs after Ben's birth, giving my youngest son a peace-filled start to his life. I'd come a long way by the time I had Ben. I was healthy, taking math and English classes with the hopes of becoming a stenographer, and blessed with this wide-eyed baby in my arms. I felt so much joy and so connected with Ben the moment I saw him. It was a welcome relief after the nagging feelings that had tugged at my soul while I was pregnant with him.

I'd been consumed by the same kind of anxiety that surrounded me when my dad was fighting cancer. I hadn't felt this way when I was expecting any of my other kids, so that made it even stranger. The only way I can describe it is as a scary, nervous feeling. I couldn't shake the thought that I was going to get cancer and die. It kept hounding me through my pregnancy with Ben, no matter how much I tried to shake it. I didn't know if I was going crazy or if some kind of demon was trying to have its way with me. All I knew was that this scary feeling really got on my nerves and I needed to be rid of it. Thankfully, that feeling continued to subside as Ben grew.

■ ■ ■

When Ben was six months old, I took in my sister's three girls. Now I had seven kids to look after—four girls and three boys—in a two-bedroom house. I had to learn the ropes like every young mother, and there was plenty to keep me busy. Sometimes you'd find me on the bus with a big stroller, a diaper bag, and kids in tow.

It was almost like that old TV show *Eight Is Enough*, but with a single mom trying to keep everyone in check. I had this little-bitty Hyundai to drive us around in. I'd be going up a hill, punching the gas as hard as I could while the car sputtered loudly. I was lucky if I hit thirty-five miles per hour. But hey, we got where we needed to go.

My biggest prayer right then was for a bigger house that could accommodate the eight of us. One day while driving through Moreno Valley, I passed a large vacant home with a "For Rent" sign out front. I knew right then that this was the house that God had for me. I parked and got all of us out of the car. After leading the kids through the gate and into the backyard, I told them, "Let's lay our hands on the house and ask God to let us live here." After praying together, we went home.

As soon as I was inside, I called the number on the sign and spoke with a lady who told me more about the four-bedroom house. When I said I was interested in it, she replied that she probably would be renting it to a military family who had called her first.

I was convinced, though, that this house was God's answer to my prayers. I began trusting that he would provide it and telling him, "Thank you for my house." I was so sure this was where he wanted us to live that I stopped looking at any other houses.

One day as I drove in that neighborhood, I heard the audible voice of God for the first and only time in my life: "You got the house." I began crying and thanking him again for the house. Not long after, the landlady called me and offered me the lease. "I don't know why, but I have to give you this house," she told me. God had provided just what my family needed; more important, I believe he was preparing me to learn to trust him in times of far greater need.

At that point, I felt lucky that I'd learned how to raise kids at a young age. I had babysat starting in fourth grade, so changing diapers and feeding an infant was practically second nature to me. I was nine when my older sister had her first baby, and by the time I was twelve, she had another kid. Plus, some of my cousins had kids.

My grandma also passed some old-time remedies. For instance, she'd tell me to brown some flour in a skillet and apply that to a diaper rash to make a baby feel better. But even with all this advice and preparation, raising babies of my own was more work than I'd ever imagined.

I was still young and learning about life, trying to reconcile the mistakes I'd made to that point. I've always tried to make the best out of situations, but if I had to do it all over again, I would've gone to school first, instead of juggling school, motherhood, and a job all at the same time. Fortunately, because one of my aunts or sisters was always willing to watch my kids for me, I knew they were being cared for when I was away from them.

Yet this workload was a blessing that equipped me well for the future. I wanted to be a strong mother who could handle her business, while also raising my kids to be independent. All of my children were very active and talked at a young age. That could make them a handful at times, but it also brought me much joy to see the spark that the Lord placed inside each of them.

Ben sure sprouted fast, in both mind and body. He began walking at eight months, and once those little legs started moving, he was unstoppable. Ben loved to jump around the house doing flying karate kicks, just like the Power Rangers on TV. I'd dress my kids in all the different colors that the Power Rangers wore. Ben liked to dress as the Green Power Ranger, who was one of the fiercest fighters, and then do his karate kicks and flips around the living room. He was accurate, too. Ben was always a fast runner, the fastest I'd ever seen. He must have gotten that from his momma.

Being my fourth child, Ben had plenty of siblings to learn from. He was like a little sponge, soaking up all the language and information around him. Even at a year old, Ben's vocabulary went beyond his siblings' abilities at the same age.

When you'd talk to Ben, all his words were very clear, not like babbling baby talk. He sounded just like a grown person in a toddler's body.

Ben's little brain worked overtime, and he retained everything he heard. I'm convinced that Ben had a photographic memory. By the time he was two, I'd use him as my walking phone book. One person I called frequently was my mom's sister Beverly (who went by the name BeBe and had helped care for all my siblings and me at one time or another). I told Ben her number one time, and then, about two months later, I asked, "Ben, what was Aunt BeBe's number again?" He recited it to me like he was reading it right off a piece of paper.

Ben was a natural at video games from an early age. Around the age of two, he could already beat his older brothers at Nintendo. That would usually start a round of whining and crying from Ben's siblings, and I'd have to step in and get everyone in check. It wasn't long before Ben's brothers and cousins tried to ban him from Nintendo. Ben would cry, "I want to play! I want to play!" So again, I'd have to step in and explain that everyone should get a turn.

While Ben's love of video games wasn't any different from most little boys', I was struck by his spiritual sensitivity. From the get-go, this boy seemed to be in tune with the Holy Spirit. Ben loved church the way most kids love playing at the park. He was never one of those kids who would tug at you and whine about the service taking too long. Once the praise and worship started, Ben's tiny arms would go up and he'd start singing along and dancing. He'd sometimes say the funniest things during service. Once when we were worshiping at

New Creation with the Pughs, Ben saw Pastor Pugh at the pulpit and yelled out, "Pastor, is that you? A-men!"

On one hand, my relationship with God was growing, but on the other, I had a hard time shaking some of the distractions around me. I was sometimes a little too worldly for my own good, letting off steam from single motherhood with a bit of partying. It would be a while before I was living fully in Christ.

Our larger house had become a kind of hangout. The front room would be filled with smoke and the sounds bumping from the stereo speakers. My cousins and other family members were often over, drinking and doing a lot of other stuff we shouldn't have been doing.

Ben sure wasn't having it. He would come walking into the room, wearing his footed pajamas and rubbing his eyes. He'd stand firmly in the middle of the room and cry out, "I want to hear Jesus songs! Mom, I want to hear Jesus songs!"

Everyone would stop what they were doing and say, "What's up with this kid?" I'd have to put some gospel music on the stereo for Ben. That was the only way to calm him down so he could go to sleep. He wasn't content with the rap or R & B we listened to on the radio. Only "Jesus songs" would soothe him.

Even as a toddler, Ben helped influence my own relationship with the Lord. I saw how this little baby was connecting with God, through both music and church services, and the happiness in Ben's heart helped make the Spirit even clearer in my own eyes. Ben helped me keep focus, and I knew I needed to give more of myself to Christ Jesus.

Watching Ben—with all of his energy, intelligence, and faith—was such a joy. That nervous, scary feeling that pestered me through pregnancy had drifted away. I was finally feeling some peace.

All that changed in an instant. Ben liked to sleep with me in my bed, and we were tucked in together one summer night in 1994 when he rolled over into me. I was jolted awake. I noticed that the clock read 3 a.m. Then Ben turned toward me, lifting his little head, and slowly opened his eyes.

What I saw made my soul feel sick. That nervous, scary feeling washed over me like never before. Something was very wrong with my baby.

CHAPTER 5

A DEVASTATING BLOW

Oh no! I thought to myself. *What's happened to my baby's eye?*

I looked into Ben's face, and my stomach twisted in knots.

I turned on the light to get a better look—Ben's right pupil was completely white. It looked like the pupil had disappeared, except for a thin line that stretched across the middle. He lay there calmly, blinking a little, like nothing was wrong. As I looked closer, the eye seemed even more ghostly. It had an eerie, fluorescent shine to it, like a toy marble or a cat's eye glowing from a light shining on it.

What is wrong with my baby? I cried to myself, examining the eye over and over again. I prayed this was nothing but a bad dream.

Ben turned over and went back to sleep. He didn't seem to be in any pain, which relieved me a little. But as for me, I was going to be up the rest of the night, too nervous to sleep and knowing I'd have to get him to a doctor.

I'd recognized something odd in the way Ben looked during the previous week. I'd noticed him turning his head to the left a lot, like he was seeing with only one eye. I didn't think much of it. Two-year-olds have all kinds of quirks, and Ben played and ran around as much as usual. That was enough for me to figure he was okay. The glow in Ben's eye had first appeared about three days before, but it was faint at first. The glow wasn't in the eyeball but seemed buried deep in the pupil. I showed this to my aunt BeBe and asked her if it looked weird. She tried to check it, but you know how tough it is to keep a two-year-old still. We couldn't tell what it was or if anything was really wrong.

The previous Sunday, Sister Devon had also noticed the weird glow in Ben's eye. She saw how the glow frightened some people at church, who thought it was some kind of demonic thing. Sister Devon insisted that I get Ben's eyes checked.

I hadn't done that yet, but once Ben's eye turned white in the middle of the night, that was it. We were soon on our way to see Ben's pediatrician in Moreno Valley.

I had never liked doctor's offices or hospitals. They reminded me too much of all the sad times we went through when my dad was sick. Hospitals meant disease and death. That nervous, scary feeling clung to me in the waiting room, but I wasn't going to let Ben know that I was worried.

Ben's pediatrician said she'd never seen anything like this before and that we had to get to a specialist right away. Now my nerves were really frazzled. She referred us to an ophthalmologist in Riverside so we could get a better idea of what was going on. We hurried right over.

The eye doctor in Riverside told me that thirty different things can turn a pupil white, but he wanted to check first for tumors. Hearing that *T* word just about made me sick. The doctor explained that Ben would need a CAT scan and that he'd need to be sedated so he wouldn't move. Although they set up the procedure right away, things did not go smoothly. The nurse tried to sedate Ben using a suppository, but it didn't work. We were told to come back the next day so Ben could be put to sleep and undergo a full-body MRI scan. This sounded like a serious procedure, and I was more nervous than ever about the results.

I didn't want Ben to soak up my fears, even though they were going to stick needles in his tiny arms and bombard his body with a powerful magnetic field from the MRI machine. There's also a risk whenever someone undergoes full anesthesia, but the MRI scan can make some people really claustrophobic and uneasy. I just wanted Ben to be comfortable and keep still so the procedure wouldn't have to take any longer than it should.

I figured the best way to prepare Ben was to appear totally happy and confident. As we left for the MRI, I said in my perkiest voice, "You know, baby, it's going to be all right!" Ben was too young to understand the gravity of the situation, even with all the doctors and imposing medical machines surrounding us. All I could do was comfort him when the doctors had to draw blood, or try to make him laugh as we waited. I had to be this little boy's hero. I had to put on the acting performance of a lifetime to keep him calm, because I felt scared to death.

Though I tried to collect my thoughts as Ben was wheeled away for the procedure, keeping my emotions in check was tough. I felt helpless and afraid. Worst of all was the uncertainty, the not knowing if things were going to be okay. It was the same kind of anxiety I'd felt when my dad was dying. The possibility that Ben might have tumors was sickening. To me, cancer equaled death.

The MRI procedure lasted only a few minutes. But, man, if you've never sat through something like that, you have no idea how tough it is. And Ben was just a baby. He'd always been such a healthy kid. There was no way I could have predicted this.

■ ■ ■

Finally I was allowed to see Ben in the recovery room. He was still sleepy from the anesthesia but otherwise seemed all right. I prayed that we weren't dealing with anything too serious. The eye doctor we'd first met with walked in about a half hour later with the test results.

The MRI showed that there were tumors in both eyes. Ben's right eye was completely consumed by a tumor; that's why it had turned white. Ben had already lost vision in that eye, and it would have to be removed. Before doctors did that, however, they needed to be sure there was no cancer outside the eye. If it spread to Ben's optic nerves, he would probably die. Chemotherapy was ordered to help keep that from happening.

The doctor explained that Ben had retinoblastoma, a cancer that develops quickly in the eye. The upside is that this cancer has a cure rate as high as 98 percent if caught early enough. About two-thirds of those with retinoblastoma have a tumor in just one eye; the other third have it in both, which is called bilateral retinoblastoma. That's what Ben had. The doctor said that, even if this cancer goes into remission, it often comes back later in life, usually when a person reaches middle age.

Bilateral retinoblastoma—the name alone sounded terrifying, and my mind started to scramble. For one panicked moment, I thought my baby had cancer because I'd named him Ben, after my dad who'd passed away. Thankfully, I shook the thought quickly. My God is bigger than that.

Knowing that Ben needed chemotherapy made me shudder. I remembered how sick that had made my dad and how he had quit doing it after just one treatment. I had a lot of questions for the doctor.

"What does chemotherapy actually do?" I asked.

"The purpose is to target all the rapidly dividing cells so we can kill the cancer cells," he said.

"You mean it's like poison?"

"No, we don't like to think of it like that."

"Doctor, you don't need to sugarcoat anything. I need to know exactly what I'm dealing with here. You're trying to make it sound like it's nothing, but this is serious."

"Yes, it is serious. We'll get moving on the treatment. We can get Ben started on chemotherapy as soon as next week."

"Oh no, we're not!" I said. "We're going to start this right now!"

The doctor couldn't really argue with me, so he checked to see if Ben could be seen at a hospital in nearby Fontana, about twenty minutes away. This was a possible life-and-death situation, and we had to move fast. I'd seen his right eye turn from a glow to ghostly white within just a few days.

I'm grateful the doctor respected my wish. This hospital agreed to take Ben right away. That night was the first of what would be many hospital procedures for Ben. He was taken into surgery so a double Hickman catheter could be inserted into his chest, through which the chemotherapy would be administered. That meant two rounds of anesthesia in a single day, which is a lot for a young child to take.

Ben was set up with his own room, which was filled with monitors and a large crib. There was also a sofa bed so I could stay with him throughout the night. This is how we'd live off and on for ten months. Every three to four weeks, we'd go back to the hospital for another round of chemotherapy. Each series of treatments kept us there for several days at a time.

Thank God I had family to keep the rest of my life in order. Aunt Cynthia took in my kids just like they were her own. My support system was phenomenal, and I never had to worry about getting help while I was tending to Ben in the hospital. I had Cynthia, I had Aunt BeBe, and I had my sister Denise. Whenever I needed someone, they were there.

The hospital sent us home with a supply of masks to keep Ben protected from germs after his chemotherapy treatments. All of the chemicals left Ben's immune system fragile, so he was more prone to getting sick than other kids were.

Keeping him healthy was tricky, especially because people were always coming and going from our house.

In March, after Ben's first chemotherapy treatments, I came home to a house full of hyperactive kids. Not only did we have seven kids in the house—four of my own, plus the three nieces who were staying with us—but one of my aunts was holding a birthday party for Tiffany and Derius. That meant another twenty or so of my cousins, nieces, and nephews were over.

Who knows how many germs were floating around that party! But I never put a mask on Ben's face. In my mind, that would have been like giving in to my fear. I knew God was in control of my baby's health. I'd always trusted God to protect us, and neither Ben nor my children got sick often from colds or the flu. Ben got sick only after his first chemotherapy treatment. In fact, he never got sick from chemo again as a toddler.

I was thankful that Ben coped well. He was never a whiny kid, and he just kept on moving despite the toxic chemicals flowing through his body. He wanted to play video games. He wanted to play with other kids. During one hospital stay, he was knocked out for two days from anesthesia and woke up on Christmas morning. Almost his first words were, "Let's go play!" I had Ben's little bike in the hospital, so I'd run down the hallways chasing after him while holding on to his IV pole. I don't know if all little kids are like that during chemo, but nothing fazed this guy.

Some things I could never get used to. Watching Ben squirm and scream while getting poked with needles was hard to take. I've always hated needles too. But the worst was seeing Ben's hair fall out. I remember rubbing his head, feeling clumps of hair starting to collect in my palms. Finally, I got a pair of clippers and shaved his little head. I even used some tape to pull all the little "pokies" out so his head would be completely clean. That's when I started crying.

The reality hurt me to the core: *My baby has cancer. . . . This is really happening. . . . I'm really going through this.* I could quit drugs. I could get my life together. But I couldn't beat cancer. I couldn't beat death. It was such a heavy feeling, like my entire world was crashing down upon me or I was walking through quicksand with heavy shoes. I felt like I'd failed my child.

Lord, how strong do I have to be? I silently prayed. *You told me you would never put more on me than I could bear. I just don't understand how much I'm supposed to take.*

Even though I'd taken control of myself, I realized that I couldn't control life. I was also in this fight alone since Stephen, Ben's father, had distanced himself from us.

Sometimes I'd have to remind myself that some parents actually had it worse than I did. In the pediatric ward, I'd met mothers who had children with terminal conditions. I felt sad for the parents of one little boy Ben's age who had a brain tumor and died. One baby girl was six months old and already undergoing chemotherapy. We never know what we'll have to face in life, but I had to remember that the Lord had a way out for me. This situation, no matter how confusing and trying it could be, was actually chosen for me. I never thought, *Why me?* but rather, *Why not me?*

CHAPTER 6

STEPPING UP FOR BEN

I HAD TO QUIT my job and school because my life now revolved around kids and hospitals. Even without a job, I was busier than ever trying to manage my kids and Ben's life-or-death medical condition. At least finding a babysitter was never too tough when Ben had a doctor's appointment or a chemotherapy treatment that would keep us at the hospital for a few days.

My hands had never been so full. But God blessed me with a big family who could help out. My aunt BeBe had been my babysitter when I was little, and now she was taking care of my own babies. Aunt BeBe had my kids picking up their rooms and running to the table when she called them for dinner. There always seemed to be a pot bubbling on our stove. She was a second mom to all of us.

Learning instantly how to be a nurse to Ben was hard,

but it had to be done. I had to make sure his catheter stayed clean, or else a potentially deadly infection could set in. Every day I had to flush the catheter with both a medicine called heparin, which prevented Ben's blood from clotting, and a saline solution. I was amazed that Ben never played with his catheter, or even with the rubber tubes coming out of his chest. He just let me do what I had to do.

This was such an unpredictable time. Just when it seemed like everything was under control, Ben would get another infection from his catheter and we'd be off again to the hospital. No matter how much we tried, keeping that catheter clean was really hard.

A mother can only take so much. Sometimes I'd sneak away and lock myself in my room. I'd get on my bed and kick and scream and holler, "Lord, I need you!" I had endured a lot in my life by this time. But I had to vent and release the pressure. I had to give it all to God. I'd have a fit for about thirty minutes, blow my nose, clean myself up, and come out like nothing had happened.

Psalm 91 became my prayer of healing during these trying times. I'd loved this passage from the time when I'd first heard it in church as a young girl:

> Because you have made the LORD, who is my refuge,
>   Even the Most High, your dwelling place,
> No evil shall befall you,
>   Nor shall any plague come near your dwelling;
> For He shall give His angels charge over you,
>   To keep you in all your ways. (verses 9-11)

The first round of chemotherapy took away a lot of that eerie whiteness in Ben's right eye. The doctors and I were so hopeful! My spirits were up, thinking Ben could beat this cancer and keep his sight. But after two months of chemo, I was devastated to find out that all the treatments and prayers hadn't been enough. The doctors ran their first MRI since Ben had started chemotherapy, and the results weren't good. The right eye was already so consumed with the tumor that the doctors decided it needed to be removed. We couldn't risk the cancer spreading to his optic nerve.

Ben was so little that he didn't understand what was going on. I felt sick inside, struggling with the thought that my baby was losing a body part and not knowing what might come next. I felt so sorry for him and so frustrated that I couldn't make it go away. But I knew I had to make this decision. It was life or death for him.

The surgery was faster than I expected, less than two hours. Pastor Pugh and Sister Devon kept me company in the waiting room. We didn't talk much. We prayed, putting our trust in God and waiting . . . and waiting.

Ben was groggy after the surgery and rested quietly in the recovery room. I put on my cheeriest face as I knelt next to him, telling him I loved him while studying the mounds of bandages that blanketed his little head. Underneath the bandages, Ben's right eye socket was deeply bruised and so puffy it closed shut. I knew this fight was just getting started.

The doctor sent us home only an hour after Ben woke up, which kind of surprised me. I figured they'd want to observe someone who'd lost an eye for a while longer. It was time to be Dr. Mom again. This was trauma on a new level for me, because I was thinking, *My baby doesn't have an eye, and I don't want to see what this looks like!* His eye wasn't just different—it was gone.

■ ■ ■

Ben's chemotherapy treatments continued after his eye was gone. And now, along with flushing his catheter daily, I had to put drops in Ben's eye socket to help it heal. During Ben's surgery, the doctor had replaced Ben's eye with a piece of clear plastic called a conformer, so he had one plastic eye and one good eye. To add the medicine, I'd have to pry open Ben's eyelid a little, try not to bump the conformer, and get some eyedrops in there. That made me really uncomfortable, so at first I drove an hour to Los Angeles to have a nurse do it for me. Then I took a reality check and figured I couldn't do that every day.

The solution, once again, was Aunt BeBe. I took Ben to her house and said, "BeBe, I can't do this! You gotta do this for me!" She was all country about it and just said, "Bring that boy here! Come here, Ben!" She added the drops like they were nothing. Each day the eye opened a little more until eventually it opened all the way up. At that point I was comfortable enough to put the drops in myself.

Ben remained a happy kid, even with his right eye gone. I was relieved that he didn't try to touch or play with his bandages. The way he ran around, you'd never know he had just one eye. He never stopped being Ben. After all, he could still see.

Though his surgery had taken care of the immediate danger, Ben wasn't cured. The doctors needed to keep a close watch on Ben's left eye as they tried to save his vision. Keeping Ben from going completely blind was our number one mission. The doctor reminded me that, even with additional treatment, Ben's cancer might come back, but if it did, it probably would not happen until he was in his thirties or forties.

The doctors ordered radiation. That meant a whole new routine. For six weeks at a time, we stayed at a hospital in Hollywood from Monday through Friday and then came home on the weekends. A close family friend named Rhonda stayed at my house to watch my kids and get them to school while Ben and I were away. Before we left for the hospital, I explained that Ben's eyes were sick and that Mom would sometimes need to be away with Ben at the hospital. My three older kids understood that.

They had a nice setup for us in Hollywood. Ben and I had a little apartment next to the hospital, and I'd push Ben across the street in a stroller when it was time for his radiation. I did my best to make this time fun for Ben, almost like we were on a little vacation. After each day's treatment, I'd take Ben somewhere, maybe to see the animals at the Los Angeles Zoo or to play at Griffith Park.

We certainly cherished those little breaks. Each treatment lasted only about sixty seconds, but they'd have to put Ben under anesthesia each time so he wouldn't move. At first they again tried using an anesthetic suppository, but they'd have to hold Ben down while he was kicking and screaming.

I couldn't take it. That was some horrible stuff for a little boy who wasn't even three years old. After two weeks, I demanded that Ben either get full anesthesia or we were going to stop everything right then.

■ ■ ■

Almost a year had passed since Ben lost his right eye. To the best of my ability, I got used to the idea that he was always going to look different from most people. I was comforted that at least he could still see. Ben never slowed down, even with just one eye. I thought of children who had it much worse than Ben. He was smart and full of life, and he was going to make his mark on this world.

Then my worst fears came true.

The doctors ran a series of tests after Ben's radiation treatments. They showed me the images, which revealed that a tumor in Ben's left eye had mutated. Instead of remaining one large tumor, it had spread inside the eyeball and showed up as a bunch of little dots. The doctor told me I could try to save his eye by going to Mexico for experimental treatments, but the consequences could be deadly if they didn't work. The other option was to remove Ben's left eye, leaving him completely blind. I kept looking at the chart, with all those dots looking like little lights.

Losing your sight is about the most devastating thing a person can go through, and this would be happening to Ben at a very young age. Plus, there was more to it than being blind. What would he look like with no eyes? Would people think he was a freak? What would life be like when he knew there was no chance he could ever see again? That put the decision on a whole other level. I was terrified, but I wasn't willing to risk Ben's life trying to save his remaining eye. I kept wondering if my choice would be the right one. After the doctors explained the options, the decision was up to me. I had to put a lot of trust in both those doctors and myself. More than anything, I had to give it to God.

My biggest worry was my boy asking me one day, "Mom, why did you let them take my eyes?"

I cringed at the thought of no girls ever liking Ben or of him being treated as an outcast at school and elsewhere. The bottom line was this: He'd been born a black male. Now he'd be a black male who was blind. That was two strikes. And if I coddled him too much, that would be three strikes and out for this kid. What would society do with this blind black boy?

■ ■ ■

There was no way I'd let Ben be like Doug.

Doug was a blind kid I'd known in sixth grade. I shared a class with Doug only during that one school year. I wasn't sure how he became blind or if he was born that way. Nobody asked, and Doug didn't say. Doug never said much of anything. He always looked so lonely and sad. He never played with the rest of us kids, and he never talked unless we spoke to him first. I don't remember him ever laughing.

Doug never touched a monkey bar or tetherball, and he stayed off the blacktop most of the time. I wonder if Doug even wanted to know what a tetherball felt like. Even the simplest joys, like playing a game of tag, were something he'd never know. It makes me sad to think about it. No kid deserves to miss out on his or her childhood.

It was my nature to stick up for people, like the time I'd defended the girl with the dirty clothes when a boy started taunting her. I wanted to stick up for Doug, too. I took it upon myself to learn more about him, and I tried to help him if he'd let me. I'd ask him a lot about braille and wonder if he could really read a book just by feeling dots. The braille books looked fascinating to me.

Sometimes I'd take Doug's arm and lead him around the playground. Looking back, I wish I would've done more for him. I would've helped him feel things, like the tetherball or those monkey bars. Maybe I could've helped him climb a tree or taught him to ride a bike.

I never saw Doug after the sixth grade. I always wonder what happened to him and if he ended up becoming successful in life. I truly hope so. But it didn't seem like he got to experience much during his childhood. I could tell by Doug's personality that he'd been overprotected and raised to be too cautious. It was like he was stranded in a world all by himself.

I'm convinced that Doug was there in my life all those years ago to prepare me to be the mother I needed to be for Ben. All those memories of Doug came racing back to my mind once I realized my own son would be blind. But I decided that I wouldn't let him miss out on things like Doug had. Ben was going to be different. He would run, play, ride a bike, and learn to fight back if he had to. I was confident that Ben was up for the challenge. No matter what medical procedures he'd gone through, nothing seemed to drain his energy or lessen his curiosity for the world. Ben's life force was strong, and I'd see to it that he remained that way. I never wanted him to ask, *What does it feel like to climb a tree? What does it feel like to ride a skateboard?* Ben was going to know. Ben wouldn't just survive—he would thrive.

CHAPTER 7

GOD'S PROMISES

Once the doctors determined that Ben needed to have his left eye removed, everything went really fast. There was no "Let's do this next week or next month." We had to beat this cancer right away, before it beat Ben.

We'd done all we could to prepare my baby for losing his eyes. A woman from an institute for the blind in Los Angeles had been working with Ben, visiting three times a week to teach him shapes and prepare him for preschool. Sister Devon brought a backpack filled with crayons and paper to the hospital, teaching him the different colors and praying that he'd remember them once his eyes were gone.

Ben was still a toddler, just shy of his third birthday, so it was hard for him to understand how much different his life was about to become. I tried explaining to him that his eyes were sick and that the doctors were making sure the rest of him didn't get sick too. I said they were going to remove his eye and he wouldn't be able to see anymore. I tried covering his left eye with my hand to show him what it would be like once he'd lost his sight. He just pushed my hand away.

Preparing myself for Ben's blindness—well, I don't even know if anyone can truly prepare for something like that. It was hard to accept that his eyes would never open again. I put my faith in knowing that he would live. And I was determined that he wasn't going to see me cry.

On January 14, the morning of the surgery, I huddled in the waiting room with Pastor Pugh and Sister Devon. Together we prayed for Ben. Slowly, my heart began to fill with overwhelming hope and love, as if I were being touched. I knew the Lord was speaking to me, not with a voice but through his presence. The Lord spoke three things to me:

> *Ben will live and not die.*
> *Ben will see again.*
> *And this isn't for you.*

The first part was easy to understand. The Lord had spoken to me all along during Ben's journey with cancer. Even though I was young in Christ, I had faith that Ben was going to live and not die.

As for seeing again, I was excited that a miracle would be revealed. I felt like I was waiting on a bang—a bolt of thunder that would come down from heaven and restore Ben's sight. Based on the Lord's words to me, I figured that Ben's eyes would somehow literally grow back. God told me Ben was going to see, and I trusted that, even if others didn't at first. When I told Aunt BeBe that Ben was going to see again, she said, "Girl, you're crazy!"

For a long time I didn't understand the part about "this isn't for you." That promise wouldn't make sense until years later, when I saw the impact Ben had on people around the world.

All I could do was trust in God as the surgeons did their work. Like Ben's first operation, this procedure took less than two hours. The hard part was facing Ben in the recovery room. I was so scared before being called back there that I was nearly hysterical. I wondered if Ben was going to look scary without his eyes. I wasn't sure of the best way to comfort him. Should I cry with him? Should I put on my best brave face?

Sister Devon held me and ministered to me so I could gather my strength before I saw Ben. She said it was important that Ben didn't sense my fears. I needed to be rock-solid to help strengthen him. Even though Ben didn't have eyes now, Sister Devon reminded me that he was full of life. He'd still be able to do many things. Transferring the strength of God to Ben could be my gift to him.

I was ready. I walked into the recovery room and saw my little boy, who was still hooked up to IVs and other machines. He was awake, but so scared and confused.

"Oh, Mom, I can't see anymore!" Ben cried to me.

I let love guide me past the fear and sadness I felt inside. I was ready to carry his burdens, to be his eyes if I had to, and to pray that my happiness would bring light to his newly darkened world. I reminded him that people see in so many different ways, through their touch, their ears, their noses. I let Ben know that his mom would always be there for him, that my love was forever.

Ben's breathing started to relax, and soon he was falling asleep. Seeing Ben find peace helped reinforce my own belief and hope that we would be okay. My boy had been through two cancer surgeries in less than a year. Now, I thought, he was safe. The doctors believed Ben would be grown before facing any risk that the cancer might return. I could finally take a deep breath of my own.

Ben's tranquility was only temporary. Later that night, he cried out again, "I can't see anymore! Oh, I can't see anymore!"

I reassured him again, letting him touch, hear, and smell me, encouraging him to paint a picture of me using his senses.

"Baby, yes, you can see. You can see me with your nose. . . . You can see me with your ears. . . . You can see me with your hands. You will always be able to see me!"

Ben finally understood. That was the last time in his life he ever told me that he couldn't see.

■ ■ ■

Ben showed his determination to live without eyes on the first morning back at the house. He started with the staircase. He held on to the railing, walked up a step, and then stepped back down. Then he went up two steps and stepped down twice. Once Ben was comfortable with that, he went up one step and jumped back down. Then he went up two steps and jumped. From then on he kept stepping and jumping. Ben immediately started figuring out space and playing like he normally would, even though his face was still swollen and covered with bandages. For the first month after becoming completely blind, Ben would crawl on his knees with his hands outstretched, feeling his way around the house. He might have looked like a baby again by crawling on the floor, but in reality, Ben was doing work.

Soon he had a good idea of where everything was in the house. He'd walk into the bathroom and immediately know where to find the sink. It's like Ben's brain was still seeing, still as active as ever. Anytime Ben was done playing with his little toys in the family room, he'd hide them under the couch, or maybe behind the pillows or cushions. When he was ready to play with his toys again, he'd know right where he'd left them. He already knew what to do so nobody else would find his toys. That was cool. He was putting his world together in order to see in a new way.

Ben was well prepared for this journey. As crazy as it sounds, he was almost excited to be blind. Every day I'd say to him, "Your name is Benjamin Underwood, and you can do anything!" And he'd smile really big, raise his little hands, and answer, "Yeah!"

■ ■ ■

The doctors told me not to take Ben out of the house until six weeks after his second surgery. I actually took him along on an errand less than a week after the operation. I wanted him to start getting comfortable in public.

Truth be told, Ben was a freaky-looking kid as he was healing, because of those clear-plastic conformers in his eyes. The sight of him scared kids sometimes. Other times, I sensed people staring at us, or they'd move away if we got too close.

People don't always know what to say to someone who's disabled. I did my best to make them feel comfortable. If I could tell someone was curious about Ben's face, I'd say, "Oh, he had cancer in his eyes and needed to get them removed." This was our life, and I wasn't going to hide a thing.

I worked with Ben so that he'd carry himself like a sighted person. I'd seen how some blind people sway their heads or rock back and forth. But right away I told Ben, "You sit up straight and keep your head straight. When you're talking to people, you look them right in the eye."

So when people talked to Ben or tried to get his attention, he always turned his head like he was looking straight at them. That threw some people off. He was so alert and on point that it seemed like he could actually see. If you saw Ben from a distance, you wouldn't think anything was different about him.

I wanted Ben to live in the most vivid world possible. When we went shopping, I would tell him what everything was. I let him run his hands along the rows of cans. I asked him to touch all the different fruits and vegetables and feel the coldness from a bag of frozen peas. If Ben knocked something over and we got some funny looks, I'd say to the people around us, "Oh, I'm sorry. He's blind." I'd always get a compassionate response, which was a green light for me to encourage Ben to continue seeking and exploring.

When it was time to go, I'd start snapping my fingers, saying, "Come on, Ben, it's time to leave." He'd come bouncing from wherever he was and grab hold of my back pocket. That's how we kept track of each other.

I was also determined to keep Ben's world full of color. Wherever we went, I described our surroundings. I'd have Ben touch things so he could paint a picture of them in his head.

"Ben, feel the leaves on this tree. This is a pine tree. Can you feel those sharp needles? Put them in your hands and smell them. That's the smell of pine, like that cleaner we use for the bathroom. Now feel this tree. Put your arms around that fat trunk. You can tell by how big it is that it's a very tall tree."

We'd touch rocks, flowers—everything he could reach. I described colors, too.

"Red is like fire, Ben. It's a hot color. It's brilliant. Blue is the color of the sky and the ocean. It's a cool color. Feel this cotton. The clouds in the sky are white and look puffy like this cotton. But sometimes the clouds get dark because they're full of rain.

"Ben, feel the sidewalk. Do you feel all the little rocks in there? Now put your hands on the driveway. Do you feel how smooth that is? That's pavement, and it's black and smells stinky when it's new and hasn't dried yet. Take your shoes off, and let's walk onto the grass. Feel how that green grass tickles your feet? Sometimes the grass gets too long and we have to cut it."

One day Ben asked me what the wind looked like.

"Baby, that's a good question. We can't really see it, but we can feel it. We can tell there's wind because we see and hear trees and branches moving. If we put a kite in the air, we know there's wind because it will lift the kite high in the sky. Hold up your hand and touch the wind. See how you can feel that tickle against your skin? That's the wind. I can't see it either. It doesn't have a color. But you can feel it's there."

I was determined that Ben was going to see the world— and he saw it. I knew it was important for him to be independent. If anything ever happened to me, Ben needed to be able to take care of himself. Nobody on this earth would ever treat him like his mother did. There was also the simple fact that I had two jobs and was raising him and my three other kids as a single mom, which meant Ben would have to handle a lot of his own business.

No matter what, Ben was going to have the confidence that "anything you can do, I can do better." It might take a little more work for him than it did for other people, but I knew Ben wasn't going to stop until he achieved something. I refused to accept that Ben would be blind even though he physically had no eyes. I refused to call him "my blind son" or remind Ben that he was blind. No. It was, "Ben, go play. Just watch out for cars. Your name is Benjamin Underwood, and you can do anything!"

There wasn't going to be any pity party in my house. I wasn't going to let Ben be crippled by fear. I also decided to live my own life with joy. Part of that was just accepting my situation. I couldn't give Ben his sight back. All I could do was my best, while trusting that God knew what he was doing. Then and now, the joy of the Lord is where my strength is, whether I'm worshiping in church or praying by my bedside.

Yes, the surgery ordeals had been draining and scary, and who knew what the future would hold for a boy with no eyes? But I still had my son. He was done with treatments, and we could start loving life again. We just had to learn how to live that life without eyes.

■ ■ ■

Once Ben's left eye socket had fully healed, about six weeks after his second surgery, we had a set of prosthetic eyes made for him. Ben would go through five pairs of them as he grew and his eye sockets got bigger. Every several years, he'd need to be fitted with a new pair. Otherwise, his prosthetics would have fallen out. His daily routine began with washing his prosthetic eyes and fitting them into his sockets. Sometimes I'd walk into the bathroom and notice that it looked as if Ben were holding actual eyes in his hands.

This seems funny looking back, but when the doctor showed me the different eye colors I could pick for Ben, I wanted them to be blue. Ben originally had beautiful dark-brown eyes, so this new color combination would have looked weird. The doctor asked Sister Devon to have a little talk with me about choosing a better color for Ben. I guess I wanted to give him something special after all he'd been through, but maybe that wasn't the best decision. I finally picked a color that was more natural-looking for Ben: hazel brown. Everyone said his new eyes looked perfect.

Soon after Ben got his prosthetic eyes, he started pre-school. I wanted my son to grow up as normally as possible, so I enrolled him in a regular preschool with sighted kids. What I didn't understand at the time was all the services Ben was going to need along the way. He'd need someone to teach him braille, as well as a mobility instructor and someone who could prepare his assignments in braille.

■ ■ ■

Meanwhile, our family continued to grow. I gave birth to another son, Isaiah, about six months after Ben lost his second eye. My relationship with Isaiah's dad had been brief, and he didn't stay in our lives. I didn't regret having my fifth child for a moment, but I did realize that these short-term romantic relationships weren't good for my kids. I knew they weren't part of God's plan for my life either. From now on, I determined, my focus would be on my children.

Since I had a newly blind son and a newborn baby, it might seem like this must have been an extraordinarily rough time. But thankfully my family was always there to help out.

I loved watching Ben bond with his new baby brother. When Isaiah came home from the hospital, I put him on Ben's lap. I always wanted my boys to feel like equal brothers, not that one was any different from the others. Ben always had his baby brother, and they were close from day one.

The greatest gift in life is love, and Ben's siblings really reached into their hearts and stepped up for him. Derius taught Ben how to find the seams on his clothing, the tags on his shirts, and the heels of his socks. He even taught Ben how to ride a bike without training wheels. That was fine with me. All kids should ride bikes. Tiffany and Joe also looked after their little brother, making sure he had enough to eat and lending him a hand whenever he needed help. Watching them take care of Ben made me think of the Bible passage from John 15:13: "There is no greater love than to lay down one's life for one's friends" (NLT).

I sometimes wondered if my youngest son, Isaiah, even realized that Ben was blind when they were little kids. He'd play with Ben like with any other kid. They'd wrestle and chase each other around the backyard. Isaiah would even speak to Ben like he was sighted, saying things like, "Ben, look over there!" or "Hey, let's watch TV."

Ben and Isaiah would get in tussles, as all brothers do. One time, when Isaiah was about three and Ben was six, we went to watch their sister, Tiffany, play soccer. Ben brought his favorite Matchbox cars, but Isaiah didn't bring any toys with him. Of course, once the game started, Isaiah wanted what Ben had.

Isaiah snuck up behind Ben, grabbed a car, and took off running. After he got away, Isaiah stopped in the grass and got real still, like a little statue. As I watched them, I noticed some of the other soccer parents looking to see what would happen next.

Ben crouched down and turned his head, leading with his ear as if to say, "Oh no, you don't!" And the next thing we knew, *boom!* Ben ran straight to Isaiah and snatched the car out of his hand. I had to laugh. That's when I knew Isaiah had figured out Ben was blind. And though Isaiah quickly realized that he wouldn't be able to get away with anything, that didn't keep him from trying.

I enjoyed watching the two boys bond in some interesting ways. When Isaiah was still quite young, Ben would ask him to spell out words for him whenever they were playing a new game. Ben would tell Isaiah what the letters spelled, which enabled Isaiah to begin reading on his own. And like me, Isaiah often described their surroundings whenever he and Ben were together.

That didn't mean dealing with Ben's blindness was always easy, especially for his older siblings. Each one grieved in his or her own way. When Derius was about eight, I found him crying on the front porch one afternoon. He was holding on to the steps as tears flowed down his face.

"Ry-Ry, what's the matter?" I asked.

"Ben can't see!"

"Baby, that's okay, you can help him see!" I said. "Look at the way you've been helping Ben learn to take care of himself. You're like another set of eyes for him, and that's a great thing. Just keep on being a good brother and helping him!"

It made me a little sad that Derius was hurting, but I felt comforted in knowing that he had such empathy for his brother. Ben was lucky to have such great siblings.

CHAPTER 8

BEN CLICKS WITH THE WORLD

WE DIDN'T KNOW what to think of Ben's sound at first. Ben's oldest brother, Joe, was the first to notice the clicking. Once Ben's other siblings picked up on it, they all started getting annoyed.

It began as a game. Ben would find one of his toys and throw it across our family room. Then he'd start clicking with his tongue, keeping his ear close to the carpet, and crawling across the floor until he found the toy.

Ben played this game over and over again. Joe-Joe would get all irritated and say, "Ben, quit making that noise! Mom, make him stop!"

Of course, that just encouraged Ben to keep making it. He'd grab the back of Joe's shirt and follow him around the house, clicking all the while. Joe would get so frustrated and holler, "Mom, he's doing it again!"

Before we ever noticed Ben's clicking, I'd started doing a

lot of snapping to help him locate me. Ben's clicking later on might have been his way of imitating my snapping. In his brain, he was somehow learning to link sound with space.

When I took Ben with me to get groceries, he'd walk next to me while I pushed the cart. Sometimes he'd start exploring on his own and go farther down the aisle by himself. When it was time to move on, I'd start snapping my fingers.

"Ben!" *Snap snap snap.* "Come on, let's go!"

"All right, Momma, I'm coming!"

Snap snap snap. "Come on, Ben, you're almost there."

Ben would come skipping down the aisle, following the sound, until he was right next to me again.

It didn't take long for Ben to start doing some amazing things. After all, I'd remind him every day, "Your name is Benjamin Underwood, and you can do anything!"

One morning I was holding hands with Ben as we crossed the street. Coming to the sidewalk on the other side, I was about to hoist him over the curb so he wouldn't trip.

Well, this boy was one up on me. Before I had a chance to say or do anything, Ben stepped over the curb like it was nothing. I did a double take. I wondered how he knew when to step over the curb, but I just smiled and thought, *Okay, Lord. This is all right, and I'm not going to question it.*

Back at home, Ben was tearing around the house like any other kid. He never used his hands to guide himself along the walls. By making his clicking sound, Ben could tell where the corners were. He could sense from clicking how long or narrow a hallway might be. He knew if a door was open or closed by the way it sounded to him.

"Look, Mom! I'm playing hide-and-seek with Derius!"

"Boy, you know there's no running in this house! Take it out in the backyard. And if you skin your knee, you better not come crying to me!"

I don't believe Ben was trying to show off. He was simply figuring out what he needed to do so he could play with his siblings. Ben was child number four, which meant he had a lot of keeping up to do. He didn't get any breaks. It wasn't going to be, "Oh, you poor thing. Just sit down. We'll take care of everything for you."

Ben developed a great attitude. He never acted pampered or tried to make others do things that he could do for himself. When Ben needed to go to the bathroom, he'd make his way through the house, find the bathroom, and do his business. I put Ben's food on the table like everybody else's. He'd figure out where it was, find his fork, and start eating. Lord knows I wasn't going to spoon-feed him. If Ben left his bowl on the table, I'd remind that boy to wash it and put it away.

Like all my other kids, Ben was going to learn to be self-sufficient. I never told him, "Boy, you're blind." To be honest, a lot of times I forgot that Ben didn't have eyes.

■ ■ ■

As Ben was adjusting to his blindness, I knew I had to make some changes in my own life. Ben would soon turn four, and Isaiah was just six months old.

My soul craved a fresh start, and I needed to get away from some of the bad influences that were bringing me down in Southern California. The environment I was in tempted me constantly with drugs. I'd drift back into using crack, then stop. But knowing I was going to use again twisted my stomach into knots. I realized that to be the mother my children needed, I had to escape from the temptation for good. It's like God told me to leave with my family, just like Abraham. In this case, my promised land was a cul-de-sac about 350 miles north in Sacramento.

Leaving Southern California was hard. Most of my extended family still lived there. The Pughs had pretty much adopted me and the kids as their own family. Sister Devon was sad to see us leave. She cried like she was losing her own daughter when I told her we were moving. But she didn't try to stop us. Sister Devon said that sometimes you have to let the ones you love spread their wings and leave. I didn't realize how long it would be before I'd see my beloved Pughs again.

I drove our moving truck up north, through the "Grapevine" highway between Los Angeles and Kern counties and on to Highway 99. Our Chevy station wagon was hitched to the back. It needed a full brake job, which I was too broke to pay for. There wasn't much of anything to move. I'd either given most of my stuff away or just thrown it in the trash.

I was very much on my own in this new town. The only family I had in Sacramento were my brothers Ernest and Vincent. Ernest and I had been close as kids, and he had been after me to move north for a couple of years. As a single mom with five kids and hardly any income, I knew this move wouldn't be easy. I was already on welfare and receiving Section 8 housing assistance, the federal voucher program for low-income families.

We stayed with Ernest for the first two months until we could get settled on our own. I needed work, so I grabbed a phone book and started making calls. I got in touch with a local Regional Occupational Program to get some career preparation training, and then I quickly found some clerical work at an insurance office. It was only supposed to be a temporary job, but after two weeks the company hired me on a permanent part-time basis.

I cold-called some more companies, offering my services as a clerical worker. I lucked out and found more work with a foster care agency. Once a nighttime job at the Department of Motor Vehicles opened up, I left the insurance job. At the same time, I enrolled at Cosumnes River College, taking a full load of night classes. I didn't have a clear idea of what I wanted to study, so I began by taking some of the general education requirements.

I had so much on my plate: two jobs, school, and raising five kids by myself. At the same time, I held a 3.75 grade point average and was also coaching my daughter's soccer team. I wanted to change my world, and the only way to make that happen was to just do it.

Thanks to my Section 8 housing assistance, we were blessed to move into a comfortable house in a south Sacramento cul-de-sac. Let me tell you, this is how good God is: I ended up with a whole new group of friends and a support system on that street. Almost all the families in the eight or so houses there had kids. There was a married couple—a doctor and a teacher—who lived next door to us on the left. A wonderful Asian family was on the other side of us. Another woman ran her own day care center on the corner and babysat a lot of the neighborhood kids.

It felt like our own little blessed village. My kids always had other children to play with. Another neighbor would take my trash out when he took his own can to the street. He'd also cut my lawn after he worked on his own.

In hindsight, I think back and say, "Look what God did!" He never left me alone. He took care of all my needs. Everyone I could have hoped for was right there—my day care provider, a doctor, teachers, true neighbors.

Thank God I wasn't living on the street and depending on the bus to get around. A neighbor stepped up and sold me her van. She knew money was tight for me and was kind enough to let me pay off the van in $500 installments. It was a big, junky, fifteen-passenger van, but that's what I drove and I was happy to have it. It was our Mercedes for all I was concerned.

So many more good things happened after we moved to Sacramento. For whatever reason, Ben's connection with the Lord grew incredibly strong during this time. During our first couple of years in Sacramento, we attended Ernest's church, and once again, Ben looked forward to going every Sunday. I had him enrolled in the public school system, and the students sang a lot of songs during class. Every day the kids would get an opportunity to share their favorite song for the class to sing. Ben was always outgoing, so one day he raised his hand and said, "I've got a song!" The teacher said, "Okay, Ben, let's hear your song," and then Ben led the class in a Christian nursery rhyme that ends with a little chant of "Jesus! Jesus! Jesus!"

From then on, Ben's arm would shoot up every time the teacher said, "Which one of you has a song?" I even have a picture of Ben with his arm up and this big ol' smile on his face as he's about to sing. The other kids would get all excited. They'd let Ben sing the first part of the song, and at the end everyone would shout, "Jesus! Jesus! Jesus!"

One of the parents complained to the principal that a teacher was having the kids sing a Christian song in class. The principal called the teacher in and said she couldn't allow her to lead kids in this song. The teacher invited the principal to come to the class and hear the song for herself.

When that time came, the teacher said, "Who's got a song for the class today?" Of course, Ben's hand went right up, and at the end of the song, the whole class was yelling, "Jesus! Jesus! Jesus!" The kids jumped up and down laughing, and the principal had tears in her eyes to see the whole class that happy. She walked off without saying a word.

That same teacher took Ben aside one day to find out what was going on in his happy little head.

"Ben, I want to ask you something."

"What's that?"

"Ben, why are you always so happy and smiling all the time?"

"Because I have Jesus in my heart!"

"What did you say?"

"Because I have *Jesus* in my heart!"

CHAPTER 9

TWO GREAT BLESSINGS

BARBARA HAASE came into our lives shortly after we moved to Sacramento. I always just called her "Mrs. Barbara." She would prepare Ben for Head Start, a program to help low-income kids under five get ready for kindergarten. My goal was for Ben to learn in public schools, and Mrs. Barbara would give Ben some extra hands-on help as his mobility and braille teacher.

Mrs. Barbara was a veteran educator who was nearing the end of her career. She was a friendly, grandmotherly-looking lady with gray hair who liked to quilt as a hobby. She'd had some amazing experiences working with kids. Mrs. Barbara had encountered preschoolers who'd taught themselves to read, as well as a student who was both hard of hearing and nearly blind yet surpassed everyone's expectations in the classroom.

Ben was going to be a real treat for her. One of Ben's doctors had told her, "Barbara, you are going to love this kid." Mrs. Barbara learned quickly that Ben was an unusually perceptive child. She and I met with some school administrators to get a better idea of how we could best help Ben.

Mrs. Barbara started by getting Ben together with other visually impaired kids a couple of times a week to develop his social skills. She also visited our home to work with Ben and tutor him in braille. Once he was in school, Mrs. Barbara would stay in the classroom to assist the teacher with Ben's needs. She was like a friendly, grown-up set of eyes for him.

Mrs. Barbara gave Ben his first cane. The end had a little ball, and she showed him the best ways to roll it across the ground and get a feel for objects. Ben's instinct was to slap the cane on the ground, like a big drumstick. As he tapped the cane, Ben could hear echoes coming off objects near the ground. Instead of using the cane as an extended kind of hand, it became another way to make "his sound."

Mrs. Barbara and I were chatting away one day while Ben sat on the floor with my keys, jingling them like a toy. Then Ben started playing a game. He'd throw the keys backward over his shoulder, turn around, and immediately find them. Mrs. Barbara knew that Ben was on to something. He was becoming proficient in what she called "auditory localization training." This is another way of saying that Ben was able to get a sense of space and direction from sound cues.

In the classroom, Mrs. Barbara noticed that Ben learned songs exceptionally fast. He was also a spunky kid who participated in group activities with a lot of enthusiasm. She'd seen that many kids in a similar condition would be much more timid. Ben struck her as fearless.

I explained to Mrs. Barbara that Ben had grown up with a large family and was used to wrestling with his brothers and cousins like little boys do. His siblings even played math games with him, like teaching Ben square roots.

Once again, Mrs. Barbara realized that Ben was on another level when it came to using sound to navigate. She sometimes took Ben to a nearby park where there was a big, elaborate play structure with lots of bars and wooden posts. For most visually impaired kids, it was a head bump or hazard in the making.

She walked Ben underneath one of the long metal slides. It was a tight squeeze, with just a few inches between his head and the slide. As soon as he went underneath, Ben reached his hand up to touch the slide. Just by the change in sound, he could tell something was above him. That was another indication to Mrs. Barbara that Ben used sound to "see" the things around him.

Mrs. Barbara figured that Ben had some concept of space and distance since he hadn't been blind from birth. From talking to people in her field, Mrs. Barbara understood that using sound to navigate is more common among people who've lost their eyesight from retinoblastoma than among people born blind. Either way, she knew Ben was one intelligent kid. She'd worked with plenty of other blind children, but nobody tuned into sound quite like Ben did. She called these "auditory clues," which visually impaired people might use to get a sense of their immediate surroundings.

Mrs. Barbara would usually wait with Ben after school if he needed to catch the bus. If there was time, she'd do a little exploring with him. Whatever sighted people could see when they looked around, she wanted Ben to experience as well.

"Let's go check out that tree over there," said Mrs. Barbara on one of these days.

"Sounds good to me."

"We're close to the tree, Ben. Tell me when you find it."

Ben walked a few steps and clicked his tongue a few times. He quickly spun around in a circle, then stopped and pointed.

"It's there!"

"Wow, great job, Ben!"

Ben nailed the target and did that spin move for extra flair. Mrs. Barbara was amazed because she'd picked out a tiny tree. The trunk was small enough that you could wrap your fingers around it. The first time I ever heard the word *echolocation* was right after that. Mrs. Barbara told me that's how Ben had been able to find the tree.

Mrs. Barbara was also impressed by Ben's physical abilities. In kindergarten class one morning, Ben said to her, "Watch what I can do!" He stood on top of his kindergarten chair and jumped right over the back. Ben landed perfectly and then flashed one of his huge smiles.

Ben took to another of her lessons like a little Tarzan boy. Mrs. Barbara focused a lot on helping students figure out the size of rooms and various spaces. One of the blind girls who was with Ben that day didn't have a good grasp of space yet, so Mrs. Barbara encouraged her to use a cane to touch the ceiling and the walls.

When it was Ben's turn, he grabbed the doorjamb, climbed up it, and got high enough to touch the ceiling. Then he jumped to the ground.

Mrs. Barbara became like a member of our family. Since I was working two jobs, she would come to our house after school and read to Ben and Isaiah. She treated my kids like they were her own grandbabies. She even made quilts for both Ben and Isaiah. Ben's quilt is filled with characters from the Harry Potter books, which he always loved. The character Hermione and the magical sword of Gryffindor are there, plus patches with an American flag, a pumpkin, and other symbols. The letters *B-E-N* go right down the middle.

The really neat part is that Mrs. Barbara raised all the characters on the quilt so Ben could feel them easily with his fingers. I keep this quilt on my bed to this day. I will always love her and remember the many times she went out of her way to help Ben.

■ ■ ■

Mrs. Barbara wasn't the only amazing teacher in Ben's life. Mrs. Ann Akiyama taught Ben's kindergarten class. She was a petite Japanese American lady who had worked with some students with disabilities such as cerebral palsy and autism, but Ben was her first blind student.

Mrs. Akiyama was a little nervous about this at first. She had pictured someone who was going to need constant attention, which is a great challenge for a teacher who has more than two dozen children to look after. Mrs. Barbara was also assigned to work closely with Ben in the classroom, but Mrs.

Akiyama was a bit unsure about the best way to approach this situation.

Mrs. Akiyama noticed right away that Ben always had a goofy, outgoing attitude and was physically strong. Most kindergarten kids still have their baby fat and kind of flop around, but Mrs. Akiyama saw that Ben was already fairly coordinated and very muscular for his age.

She loved to watch Ben run around and laugh at a big park next to the school. He was just as free and happy as the other kids. The kindergartners treated Ben like any other classmate, a kid who liked to run fast and swing on the monkey bars.

Running around school was sometimes a little tricky for Ben. He slammed into a brick wall one day right in front of Mrs. Akiyama and banged his head pretty hard. Her heart dropped when she saw that, and she rushed over to make sure Ben was okay. Luckily, he picked himself right up. Mrs. Akiyama called me anyway to let me know what had happened. I said that as long as Ben was fine, she should just let him do his thing.

Despite the occasional head bump, Ben was very aware of the objects around him. There was an archway in front of the kindergarten classroom, and when Ben went through it, he'd say to Mrs. Akiyama, "Look! I'm going under the bridge!" That caught her off guard the first time, but she realized quickly that Ben was hyperalert and that sounds helped give him a sense of place.

Mrs. Akiyama became so fond of Ben that she helped watch him after school on some days. Ben also spent time

Ben at about eighteen months.
He was always so happy.

BEGINNINGS

RIGHT ▶

Ben recovering at home after his first surgery.
I had to be brave while he was awake, but when he slept . . .
everything we were facing would hit me.

BELOW ▼

The day after his surgery, Ben was all smiles
again. But his hair loss made me cry because
it reminded me the cancer was real.

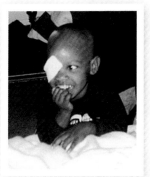

After Ben's second eye was removed, it took six weeks of healing
before he could get prosthetics. When we went out in public, some
kids were scared of Ben, but I always took the time to help them
understand that Ben's eyes were sick and the doctor had to take them
out to make him better. I refused to hide my son from the world.

Ben's siblings taught him to skate, ride his bike, play ball, and do everything else he needed in order to hang out and play with them. You're only a kid once, and I wanted Ben to enjoy his childhood.

NORMAL LIFE

BELOW ▼

Ben visiting a friend at her home. They rode horses that day and went swimming—and Ben even practiced his driving!

◀ **LEFT**

Ben practicing karate on his way to becoming a yellow belt.

RIGHT ▶

One of the only things Ben was afraid of as a child was water. But he faced that fear and learned to swim—and eventually got to swim with dolphins! He noticed that their clicking noises were even faster than his.

ADVENTURES

Ben was featured in *People* magazine!

There was the time a fifth grader thought it would be funny to punch the blind kid and run. So he snuck up on Ben Underwood and hit him in the face. That's when Ben started his clicking thing. "I chased him, clicking until I got to him, then I socked him a good one," says Ben, a skinny 14-year-old. "He didn't reckon on me going after him. But I can hear walls, parked cars, you name it. I'm a master at this game."

Ask people about Ben Underwood and you'll hear dozens of stories like this—about the amazing boy who doesn't seem to know he's blind. There's Ben zooming around on his skateboard outside his home in Sacramento; there he is playing kickball with his buddies. To see him speed down

THE BOY WHO SEES WITH SOUND

Since age 3, Ben Underwood skateboards, shoots hoops and plays video games. How does he do it? Just like bats and dolphins

"I'm a normal kid," says Ben, who lost his sight at 3 (Right, he listens for noises made by a beluga whale at San Diego's SeaWorld; left, he inspects his prosthetic eyes).

Our family on an outing to the George Washington Carver Museum.
That day, Ben met one of the last African American Tuskegee Airmen,
who was in his nineties and blind!

FRIENDS AND FAMILY

BELOW ▼
Even grocery shopping
with Ben could be an
adventure!

ABOVE ▲

The first time we met Stevie Wonder, he already knew
who Ben was. I couldn't believe this music legend had
heard of my son! My younger son, Isaiah, and I also
enjoyed spending time with Stevie.

Ben was honored with the Soaring Spirit Award from
Looking Beyond, a nonprofit that helps young people
with special needs. He spoke at the luncheon event . . .

. . . and was surprised when Stevie Wonder joined him
onstage! It was after this event that Ben and Stevie
became great friends.

Ben surfing in Hawaii, a little over a year before he died. Once a boy who was afraid of water, Ben grew into a confident young man who faced the ocean with a smile.

Carrying Ben downstairs when he was no longer able to walk.

GOING HOME

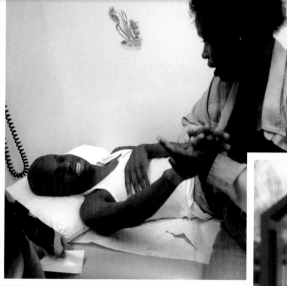

BELOW ▼

On our way to the hospital for another radiation treatment.

ABOVE ▲

When Ben's cancer returned, he and I spent long hours in the hospital talking, singing gospel songs, and praising God. He knew he was headed to heaven and told me, "You just be ready to meet me there."

Ben's homegoing celebration was on January 26, 2009,
which would have been his seventeenth birthday. It was
a day full of praise for God's work in Ben's life – and all
the light my wonderful boy brought to the world.

with her family outside of school. Mrs. Akiyama had a son who was a year younger than Ben, plus some nieces who were about the same age. That made for a perfect set of playmates. For many years Mrs. Akiyama even took Ben and Isaiah trick-or-treating with her own kids. Ben kept a hand on Isaiah's shoulder as they ran from house to house. If any of the houses had stairs leading up to the porch, Ben would always jump from the top step to the ground after getting his treat. Mrs. Akiyama was flabbergasted at first.

"Ben, you could hurt yourself from all that jumping."

"I'm going to be fine. I got this."

"Well, how do you know where to land?"

"That's easy. All I do is count the steps when I walk up them. Then I know how far to jump!"

If they'd pass a house that didn't have a porch light on, Ben would sometimes point out that they'd missed a stop. His perception of distance was really good. And once Ben dipped a hand inside his bag with all the candy, he could name each one by touch, be it a long and round Tootsie Roll or a box of Dots gumdrops.

Ben once called someone out for not putting any candy in his bag. He could tell by the lack of sound and feeling in the bag that he'd been ignored. Oh, that boy could really be a rascal! On some trick-or-treating adventures when Ben got older, the door would open and he'd say, "Want to see a trick?" Then he'd take out his prosthetic eyes!

Mrs. Akiyama also liked taking the kids to Pixie Woods, an amusement park in nearby Stockton that features a train ride and lots of other fun stuff. She'd watch Ben climbing the play sculptures, figuring out how to navigate the steps, and never shying away from anything.

One time, when Mrs. Akiyama took the kids to a large park, they stayed after the sun had gone down and the playground was completely dark. Mrs. Akiyama figured the kids now had a level playing field with Ben. She let them play in the darkness until they were all pooped out. When the kids played together inside, they liked to shoot Nerf arrow guns. Ben never had a problem hitting his favorite target: Mrs. Akiyama's son.

Mrs. Akiyama noticed that Ben was always in tune with his surroundings, picking up on sounds that others might not notice. Ben was with her at her sister's house one summer afternoon, and while sitting on the porch he said, "Ah yeah, there's a swimming pool over there." He heard the low hum from the pool's filtering system.

That street was right near the banks of the Sacramento River, and Ben tuned into those sounds as well. He'd talk about the boats he could hear nearby, the wind coming through the trees, the occasional rushing sounds of flowing river water. Sound perception became automatic for Ben.

Ben was already becoming so independent at a young age, and I'll always be grateful to Mrs. Akiyama and Mrs. Barbara for encouraging him to explore and try new things. Not only was he learning with sound, but soon Ben could tell the difference between cars and trucks by clicking alone.

He'd eventually refine that clicking technique to an extraordinary degree. And it would play a key role in reaching audiences we never dreamed of.

CHAPTER 10

PERFECTING AN INNER GPS

ONE AFTERNOON five-year-old Ben and Mrs. Barbara walked from our house to the park. She had left her car a little way down the street. As they got closer to the car, Ben came to a fence in a neighbor's front yard that ran along the sidewalk. Ben automatically put his hand out and pointed when they reached the end of the fence. Mrs. Barbara thought, *What is this kid doing?*

Mrs. Barbara wanted to test him. "Ben, we're coming up to three parked cars. Mine is on the end. Tell me when you find it."

They walked along the sidewalk and approached the cars. Ben stopped suddenly. "Well, there's the first one," he said. "Actually, that's not a car. That's a pickup truck."

Mrs. Barbara stopped and said, "Whoa!"

I had a hard time wrapping my head around the way Ben used his sound. But it was amazing. As he grew, I became more aware that he was learning to tune into our world in his own way.

Ben tried to explain to me what he saw in his head. Once he clicked, he said the sound went out in a wide direction, like a rapidly expanding circle. It's like the clicking was casting a net in which he could capture objects. Ben described a single click as turning into a bunch of rubber balls that ricocheted really fast in different directions. Depending on where those "balls" hit, Ben could sense how high the ceilings were, how near he was to a wall, or if there was a garbage can in front of him.

Ben would demonstrate. "I'm going to click down . . . *click!* That sound hits the floor, then it hits the kitchen counter. It bounces around some more, and I'm scanning everything inside my head."

The sound waves from Ben's clicking bounced off nearby objects. As Ben's brain interpreted the echoes coming back to him, he could tell the difference between a small or large room, if an object was short or tall, if a sidewalk was straight or curvy, and so much more.

I wondered how far his sound reached.

"Oh, it can go really far," Ben said. "But when you click to the sky, it never comes back. It's never-ending."

Whether he was riding his scooter, playing a game, or walking down the hall at school, I always wondered what Ben saw inside his head. I thought it might be like turning off the light in a bathroom and closing your eyes: pure darkness. When I asked him, he said, "No, Mom, don't think blindness is blackness. It's nothingness, like a big hole, like it doesn't exist."

To hear the word *nothingness* come out of Ben's mouth

hurt my heart. I didn't want him stuck in a world of nothingness. I thought Ben must be seeing some sort of color, maybe black or gray. But if you don't have eyes, I guess you wouldn't know what black or gray looks like.

That's not to say Ben's mind wasn't creating some kind of images. Ben told me that he had a "visual display" in his head, which I guess would look like some kind of computer monitor or movie screen. Even though I couldn't fully envision it, that sounded a whole lot better to me than nothingness.

Ben always paid attention to the smallest details in words and music so he could visualize them. Ben liked the Harry Potter book series, so I'd take him to see those movies. He knew all the story lines and would narrate to me as the movie went along. He'd ask me to describe what the characters looked like on the screen, and I'd say something like, "That one's a big guy who looks like Santa Claus with a big white beard and a fat belly, and he's about seven feet tall." Ben completely understood the concept. He might be blind, but he was certainly seeing something.

His determination to live without limits always made this momma proud.

■ ■ ■

As amazing as Ben's abilities were, he remained a regular kid. At age six, Ben spent his first week at Camp Okizu, a residential camp for kids battling cancer, along with their families. Every summer, Ben looked forward to this week when he could enjoy horseback riding, river rafting, ropes courses, archery, nightly campfires, and much more.

I remember the first time I took him to camp. Almost immediately, Dr. Mike, the camp physician, asked if he could take Ben hiking. I agreed and said I'd go with them. Dr. Mike hoisted Ben on his shoulders, and we set out walking. The mountains around the campground were so steep that I was quickly out of breath. I turned around and came right back, but those two continued up that mountain.

A number of pediatric oncology treatment centers in northern California are involved with the camp, so kids can continue their chemotherapy treatments under the care of nurses and a doctor while there. That became a blessing for Ben later in life. As a kid, Ben loved all the camp's activities and tried everything. In fact, he said that he first remembered clicking while learning to navigate the grounds at Camp Okizu, which he did with no problem.

Ben had few problems getting around his school either. He knew where to find all the classrooms, and he called all the teachers in them by name. He started memorizing these things from the first day of school. The trick was that some of his schools were open year-round, so every few months he'd rotate to different classrooms. It took a couple of days for him to figure out his new routine, but he just rolled with it. If Ben accidently wandered into the wrong classroom, he'd say something like, "Oh hey, I was just checking y'all out!" After that, he'd know exactly where to go.

On the elementary school playground, Ben was a firecracker. He ran around the track with the other kids, which amazed everybody. He loved to grab one of those big, red rubber balls and play four square with the other kids. Ben would win a lot of the time. This stunned me, because I can't imagine playing this game with my eyes closed. The space for playing four square is quite small, and you have to bounce the ball right inside someone else's square, or you're out. If someone knocks the ball into your square and you don't hit it back in time, you're out.

After hearing the ball bounce, Ben could immediately sense its position. Then he'd know right where to move his arms and hands to bounce it back, with either a lot of force or just enough to get the ball in another player's square. Ben's young brain was adapting quickly and getting steadily more perceptive.

But there were even more impressive skills to conquer.

■ ■ ■

Ben's video game skills astounded people, especially his brothers. Only Ben knew exactly how he could play a Nintendo DS like anyone else. I'd think the whole process depended on being able to see the action on the screen. My best guess is that he tuned in to all the little sounds and worked the controller with his fingers until he liked what he heard. Later he said he memorized the game scenarios and learned the sounds characters made before they moved or attacked. A lot of these games require great skill and concentration. Along with paying attention to the sounds, the player must memorize various button combinations on the controller. Since Ben likely had a photographic memory, he'd figure out those combinations quickly, then unleash them on his opponent.

Some people were skeptical about Ben's ability to play

video games. All I can say is that if you had the chance to go head-to-head with him, you'd see what was up.

As he got older, Ben used to bet his oldest brother, Joe, in push-ups that he could beat him at various video games. Joe came into Ben's room late one night while his brother was still up playing a fighting game called *Killer Instinct*. Ben said, "Play me, bro. I'll bet you fifty push-ups that you can't beat me." So they went at it—and Ben beat Joe five times in a row. Joe was stunned. And also bummed that he was on the hook for fifty push-ups.

Another time, Ben came flying down the stairs, yelling, "I beat *Zelda*! I beat *Zelda*!" *The Legend of Zelda* is a video game classic that's known for being very complicated. Most sighted players never win it. Beating *Zelda* means solving puzzles, using a magic compass to find your way through a dungeon, battling enemies, and much more.

Ben sometimes got help from others, who would read the maps and other instructions to him. When his brother Derius played *Zelda*, Ben liked to sit next to him, asking him lots of questions about how to make the sword more powerful and picking up other tips. Though Ben logged all that into his memory banks, it was still up to him to figure out how to put his knowledge into action. Joe couldn't believe it when Ben solved the game. No wonder Ben dreamed of becoming a video game designer!

■ ■ ■

One day, when Ben was about nine, we were walking to the grocery store, and I noticed that he was being a little quieter than usual. I could almost hear the wheels turning in his head, until he finally said something I had hoped I'd never hear.

"Mom, I wish I could see."

His words cut right through my heart. All I could do was counter his sadness with pure positivity.

"But, Ben, look at what you *can* do!" I said. "You beat everyone in video games, you ride bikes, and you have more friends than anyone I know. If there were a blackout right now, we'd all have to follow you!"

You should've seen the smile that came across Ben's face.

"You're right!" he said with a laugh. "I guess I should look at it like you do."

That's all it took. Ben never said "I wish I could see" again.

Still, it was a tough moment. One of my biggest fears was that someday Ben would ask me why I had let the doctors take his eyes. Deep inside, I'd always grappled with the guilt that I'd let my son go blind. I knew that I wasn't being fair with myself. Allowing the doctors to remove Ben's eyes wasn't a difficult decision. I didn't have any other options. Death or his eyes. I just didn't want Ben growing up thinking that he was any less of a person because he was blind. I needed him to be confident and comfortable in his own skin.

I'm thankful that the Lord placed a go-getter spirit in Ben. I'm telling you, this kid never gave up. That's how he learned to play baseball. You could pitch him a ball, and he'd hit it. He wrestled and played football with the other kids, and he hardly ever got hurt. Being an active kid, Ben eventually suffered his share of scrapes and bruises. He took a pretty bad fall while riding his bike one day with his brothers and some friends. They actually had to carry Ben home, but like always, he'd just keep on riding another day.

Men are strong vessels, and I wanted all my boys to be masculine and strong. But for a single woman, trying to raise a boy to be a man is almost an impossible task, simply because I'm not a man. It sure wasn't easy, but I did my best. I didn't want Ben to be afraid of anything, and I wanted him to do everything. That even meant learning how to defend himself.

Kids can be especially cruel, you know. That can get even worse for a child who's different physically or mentally from others.

When Ben was in kindergarten or first grade, he'd be swinging on the monkey bars, and a lot of the kids would say, "You're not blind! No, you're not!" Sometimes kids would take something that belonged to him, just to try to make him mad. Then they'd start testing him and yell, "How do you know where I'm at? Come on, find me!" Ben would tune in and just point them out without clicking at all: "Okay, you're right there, and you're right there." He'd point everybody out like it was nothing.

This went on all the time, but it kind of hurt my feelings. I didn't like how some kids would single Ben out and play with him like that. I asked Ben once if any of this bothered him. He said no, it was fun. I realized later that Ben was learning from all of these kids. These games allowed Ben to practice finding people, to really hone his sense of hearing and use of sound.

On the other hand, some kids found out the hard way that Ben wasn't going to be bullied by anybody. In fourth or fifth grade, Ben was walking home from school when a kid started teasing him about being blind. He called Ben a "blind bat" and some other mean names. Ben warned the boy to leave him alone and said, "You don't know me." The boy hit Ben on the cheek and took off running.

Ben wasn't going to just take that and get played like some scared kid. He immediately started chasing the boy. And when he got hold of that bully, Ben beat him up pretty good.

The principal at school found out about the fight, and Ben was suspended. When Ben got home, it looked like he was ready to cry. He thought he was getting in trouble. I sat Ben down to find out what happened, and he told me about the scuffle.

"Baby, you're not in trouble," I said. "I just want to know why you were fighting."

"He kept calling me a 'blind bat' and was laughing at me. Then he punched me. Mom, he made me so mad!"

"I know, Ben. How were you able to catch him?"

"When he was running away from me, I could hear the zipper on his backpack. I followed that sound until I finally caught up to him. And then I let him have it."

"You know I don't like fighting, but I'm glad you were able to take care of yourself. I don't want kids thinking they can pick on you because you're blind."

"I don't want to fight. I was just minding my own business, and he wouldn't stop messing with me. I kept saying,

'You don't know me. You better leave me alone. I'm telling you, you don't know me!'"

Ben didn't get messed with too much after that.

Ben was deeply protective of his family, especially Isaiah. Those two used to fight plenty among themselves and liked to make fun of each other. They'd always go back and forth saying stuff like, "You ugly!" . . . "No, *you* ugly!"

But when Isaiah had to deal with a couple of older bullies who were Ben's age, that didn't fly with Ben. He would always say in that strong, deep voice of his, "Y'all quit messing with him. Leave my brother alone!"

The other kids saw that Ben was no chump, and not only would he stand up to a fight, he might beat someone up in the process. Joe still remembers how Ben would stand up to anyone who was trying to bully him. When Ben was about nine or ten years old, Joe saw Ben fight in the park a few times. Some kids would tease Ben about being blind or whatever, and Ben would step up and fight. Joe always said that Ben would just demolish his opponents, even older kids.

Ben could've been a boxer. His hands were so fast, and it seemed like he could hit thirty times in a second. Someone would try throwing one punch, and he'd come back with four more—*bap! bap! bap! bap!*—and wrap somebody up. Ben would get on Joe like this when they were kids.

One time Ben was watching *Pokémon* on TV when Joe decided he wanted to watch BET. When Joe changed the channel, Ben started crying and ran upstairs. After he calmed down, Ben came back down and started whining, "Pleeeease, let me watch it!" Joe still wouldn't let him change the channel, and that got Ben really mad. Ben reached out to get a feel for Joe's face and then started firing on his older brother with his fists. That boy was something else.

Believe me, Ben was not an angry kid by nature. He loved connecting with the Lord. He loved meeting people and making friends, and when he was enjoying himself, he'd let out the goofiest laugh you've ever heard. Ben simply wouldn't allow himself to back down from a challenge. Some kids mistakenly equated his blindness with weakness, but Ben wasn't going to crawl in some corner and hide from people who wanted to take advantage of him or hurt him.

CHAPTER 11

NO LIMITS

SOME PEOPLE LOOKED at me funny when they saw how I raised Ben. Some of them straight-up confronted me. They said I was too hard on him. That I expected too much. They could say all they wanted. The last thing I'd ever do was allow Ben to believe that his life had limits, or that he was any different from other kids. My resolve only grew stronger as I saw how capable Ben was as he got older. If I got some funny looks from other parents, so what? All I know is that the Lord chose me as his mother.

Not only did I not want Ben to feel helpless, but being a single mom meant that I had to be sure every one of my kids helped keep our family functioning. By this time I was working two jobs. The first one ran from 7 a.m. to 3:30 p.m.

at the electric company in Sacramento. Then I'd work the 5 p.m. to 1:30 a.m. shift at the Department of Motor Vehicles.

I lived on about three or four hours of sleep, but that's always been enough for me. I'm naturally kind of hyper. I wouldn't try to catch up on sleep on the weekends either, because that time belonged to my kids. I didn't see them much during the workweek. Fortunately, between my older children and our neighbors, I had lots of help, so I wanted to give them all of me during my time off.

When Ben was about seven or eight years old, he had an accident on the playground at school. He loved playing out on the blacktop with his classmates. He enjoyed playing four square or tetherball—especially when he won. He liked chasing his classmates or playing tag with them. Ben was always in the mix, running around. He would sometimes get so excited and caught up in the fun that he'd forget what he was doing. I always told Ben, "Baby, just make sure you use your sound when you're out running and playing."

I got a call one morning from the school nurse saying that Ben had run into a pole and was crying. I asked if I needed to pick him up and take him to the doctor, but the nurse told me he was fine—just shaken up, mostly. I asked to speak to Ben, and she passed him the phone.

"Ben, what happened?" I said.

"I was chasing someone, and I ran into a pole," said Ben, with a little whimper in his voice. "Mom, I chipped my tooth."

"Does it hurt? Do you want me to come get you?"

"No, I think I'm going to be okay. I just wanted to catch him."

"Well, you have to be careful when you're running around at school. You know what I said about making sure to use your sound. I'm glad you're okay. Just be careful and stop crying. You're going to be all right."

It was important that all my kids learn how to take a fall. Anything that we want to do well takes practice, and there will be stumbles along the way. We might even chip a tooth in the process. I wanted Ben to play and see the world, and to be capable of getting back up and moving on whenever he fell. It hurt me that Ben ran into that pole, but at least now he knew that pole was there and wouldn't run into it again.

By the way, Ben didn't get any more cautious on the playground or decide it was too dangerous to play tag. But he never ran into another pole either. Ben just learned from the experience and moved on from there. He took his collision with the pole as a strong reminder to always use his sound and be extra mindful of his surroundings when he was running around. The last thing Ben would do was withdraw from the things he liked, whether it was riding his bike or chasing after classmates. In fact, Ben told the school principal to move the pole because it got in his way. That kid had some nerve for saying that, but I'm glad he thought that way.

As a little boy, one of Ben's only fears was water. Before he lost his eyes, he'd jump into a pool in a second. But after he went blind, it took a long time for him to get comfortable in water again. I had to keep floaties on Ben's arms for years. He didn't learn how to swim until he was eight. It hurt to see him go from jumping into a pool with no worries to being afraid. But I wasn't going to quit encouraging him until he was comfortable in the water again. I didn't want him to be afraid of anything.

When Ben finally learned to swim, none of the kids wanted to play Marco Polo with him because he could find everybody. His ability to listen became a kind of built-in sonar that made it easy for him to know exactly where the other players were.

■ ■ ■

Ben had more confidence and ambition than a lot of sighted kids. He didn't see only what was happening today—he saw the future. By the age of eight, he'd announced that he was going to be a writer. In fourth grade he started working on a fantasy-adventure novel, which he titled *Four Magical Stones*. He wrote the seventeen-chapter manuscript using his BrailleNote computer. He loved Japanese anime cartoons because he thought their story lines were really good. He especially liked Pokémon. I got him a set of Pokémon figures so he could feel their shapes. He said he wanted to design video games for a living.

Some of my favorite moments were hanging out with Ben on our couch while we watched the *Avatar* cartoon. He'd narrate to me so I could figure out what was going on, and I'd describe what the characters looked like. I'd say how the character named Aang was bald with a blue arrow tattooed on his head. There were always battles between good and bad, and Ben related to that easily. Plus, the characters had superhuman abilities that sparked Ben's imagination. I wonder if he ever fancied himself as a real-life version of an *Avatar* character.

Ben didn't spend too much time indoors, however. As he got older, he loved to ride on his Rollerblades. He'd start by building up speed on the sidewalk, and then he'd leap over the gutter and land in the street. One weekend, Ben and his two older brothers were on Rollerblades at the park. Suddenly, a dog came running from behind some bushes and started chasing them.

"That dog sounds mean!" Ben said to Joe.

"Hurry up and grab my arm," said Joe.

"I'm trying. Don't make me fall!"

"He's getting closer! Keep your legs straight and hold on tight!"

"I'm good. Go, Joe, go!"

The dog soon gave up the chase, but those boys rushed all the way home, out of breath and laughing.

While Ben escaped from that dog, he did end up with a scar on his forehead while taking running jumps over a big pillow from the couch. During one attempt he jumped too far and hit his head on the corner of the TV stand. Oh my, it was a big ol' gash, and Ben had to get stitched up to stop the bleeding. I reminded Ben to always measure his space and always—always!—use his sound. Getting stitches was no fun. But Ben was just a kid teaching himself about space and distance, and I wanted it to stay that way. It wouldn't be fair if he had to sit on the sidelines while everyone else played. Even if I had told him to, it's not like Ben would have sat still anyway.

Still, I learned fairly early that other parents would sometimes think I was being irresponsible. During the fall we spent a lot of weekends at my daughter's soccer games. Tiffany was always very athletic, and I liked to go cheer for her from the sidelines while Ben found some monkey bars or other kids to play with.

At one game, I realized I'd left some paperwork at home that I was supposed to give to the coach. We only lived about four blocks away, so I did what any other parent would have done. I let my ten-year-old son play in the park for a few minutes while I went to get the papers. Other parents were there watching their kids, so I had no worries.

I walked over to the monkey bars and said, "Ben, I'm going to run home. I'll be right back. You just stay at the park." I left Ben there with his little brother, and of course nothing bad happened.

Let me tell you, a couple of parents on the team were not happy. When I came back, they gave me funny looks, like *I can't believe she really left him!* I was thinking, *Why are they treating Ben like he was helpless or something?*

In time, we were all good. For the rest of the season, I got to know these parents better, and they learned more about Ben. I explained how he could see by clicking, that he loved playing Nintendo games and riding bikes, and that he was just another kid. The only thing different was his way of seeing. Once they knew that, the parents started to soften, and I could tell that they didn't see me as some crazy mom anymore. In fact, we ended up becoming friends. We talked later about those first impressions, and one of the soccer moms laughed and admitted, "Well, I saw you leave this boy at the park, and I thought, *What is wrong with this lady? She's leaving this blind kid here alone?*"

Even some of my family members still needed convincing that I was raising Ben properly. I'm thinking of one particular cousin, Kello, who moved to Sacramento about three years after I did. She hadn't seen us in a long time, and when we finally connected, she was astonished by Ben's abilities. He was outside playing with all the other kids in the neighborhood, running around the house—all the usual stuff young people do. We had an interesting heart-to-heart talk that day.

"I used to be mad at you," Kello confessed to me. "Before you left Southern California, I always thought you were too hard on that boy. I always thought you should have babied him more and kept him closer to you."

"But he's a kid, and kids need to play," I said. "He's a perfectly able kid and doesn't need to be treated like we feel sorry for him."

"Well, if he was my baby, I guess he'd still be handi-capped," she said. "I'd still be spoon-feeding him. But I see how Ben is now. I guess you were right all along."

We finally laughed about it. I'd never thought of myself as a harsh mother, but I guess some people felt I was sup-posed to hold Ben like a little baby and keep him away from other kids.

Whether or not he had eyes, I needed Ben to have confi-dence in himself. I needed him to think, *Whatever comes my way, I can do this.* Once they got to know him, the skeptics realized that Ben could see, in his own way. Ben was raised to take care of himself. He was an able-bodied kid who didn't need his mommy holding his hand 100 percent of the time. That's why the naysayers didn't faze me at all. As his mom, I knew that Ben's capabilities were beyond those of most kids, sighted or not.

Look, everybody wants to tell people who are handicapped what they can't do. I wanted to be the one to tell Ben what he *could* do—and as I said before, every day I'd remind him, "Your name is Benjamin Underwood, and you can do anything!"

■ ■ ■

Some people gave me and Ben funny looks—not because they were judging us, but because they couldn't figure out how Ben was able to "see." In fact, most people didn't even know right away that Ben was blind, especially since he never used a cane. Ben had some neighbor friends who didn't realize he was blind for the first week after they met. The muscles inside Ben's eye sockets still worked, so when Ben played video games, his prosthetic eyes would move back and forth slightly, just like the eyes of anyone else who was following the action on the screen. I'd had Ben practice moving those muscles when he'd first lost his eyes, though over time he couldn't move them as well as before.

Ben would've been the same kid to me whether he had eyes or not. I just don't believe in trying to put people in little categories. We spend so much time focusing on how different we are, whether it's the color of our skin, our political beliefs, or whether we get around in a wheelchair or with a cane. At the end of the day, we're all going to live, and we're all going to die. We're really not that different. That's why I don't like using the term *disabled*. It's just another way of separating people.

A lot of people were awestruck by Ben, to the point of sometimes feeling freaked out. When people discovered that Ben was blind and saw him riding a bike, they would just stop and stare for about a half hour, trying to figure it out. I heard so many people say, "He sees shadows or something, right?" Some people would put their hands in front of Ben's face and say, "How many fingers am I holding up?" And Ben would say "one" or "four" or whatever it was. He would get it right every time. It was weird to me, too, but I didn't doubt anything.

I know that with Christ we can do all things (Philippians 4:13). We limit ourselves because we can't see beyond what's in front of us. It's like if we see a wall, we stop right there. We don't take the next step and realize that something might be on the other side of that wall. We can't see past it, so that's where our determination ends. But God wants us to see beyond that, because he is able to do everything we imagine in the most exceeding and abundant way (Ephesians 3:20). We can't even fathom what God has given each and every one of us.

As a parent, I think we need to teach each of our children to be his or her own person. It wouldn't have been fair to hold Ben back from the momentum he was already creating in life.

I loved having Ben as my little sidekick while running

errands and everything else. I wasn't going to be the kind of mom who'd make Ben stay home, fearful that other people might give funny looks to this blind kid, or worried that he would get overwhelmed in public. Nope, that wasn't me. If there were errands to run, Ben was coming along. Life wasn't going to stop for either of us. At the same time, I needed to know that Ben could take care of himself. Sometimes that meant leaving Ben at home while I handled my own business.

A lot of parents tell me that they wouldn't be able to let a blind child move so freely in the world like I did. I say, why not? The world is so big, and blind people can see—they just see differently. Parents let their sighted kids ride their bikes every day in the street. They fall down. They get broken arms. Being Ben's mother meant allowing him to fall, just like we all do, so he could become the total person the Lord intended him to be. One of the most important lessons in life is that falling is okay. You've got to get back up. When the rain comes, you just grab an umbrella.

CHAPTER 12

DOING WHAT KIDS DO

WE MOVED when Ben was in fourth grade. Even though our new house was not too far from our old one, Ben and Isaiah would be going to a new school.

On our first Sunday at the new house, I took Ben and Isaiah for a walk to show them the new route to school. "Okay, Ben, when you walk out of the house, you're going to turn left on Delage. When you come to the corner of Delage, you'll be at Vintage Park. Then you make a right. The first street you'll cross is Bugatti." We continued walking along Vintage Park, and I named each street we crossed on the way to school. "This is Benz Court . . . and now this is Stutz Court. . . ." The walk was about five blocks. At last, we arrived at the school.

As we walked back home, I pointed out a fire hydrant at the crosswalk. "That'll take you right back to Delage," I told Ben. I asked him to touch it with his hand.

"Now remember this fire hydrant," I said. "This is exactly where you need to cross when you come to school Monday. The school's right there. You'll need to remember this route for coming home, too."

That Monday, I told my boss I needed to leave early because my kids were walking home from school for the first time and I wanted to see how they did. He'd met Ben plenty of times before, so he was happy to let me go.

I parked about a block from the school and hid behind a trash can. The bell rang, and all of the kids, including Ben and Isaiah, came pouring out of the school. Ben was using Isaiah as a guide, his arm around Isaiah's little shoulder. As they were walking, Isaiah came to a sudden stop.

"Ben, that looks like Mom's car!" he said.

"Whatever, Isaiah, just keep walking," said Ben.

I was across the street still hiding behind that garbage can and cracking up because it *was* my car. But they kept walking. Once they reached the fire hydrant, Isaiah stopped and turned his head really slowly, being careful to look for cars.

"Come on, Isaiah. Nothing's coming," I heard Ben say. "Let's go."

They crossed the street and kept on going toward our house. I just laughed to myself and thought, *Those boys are going to be just fine.*

■ ■ ■

Ben met some resistance at his new school that he hadn't encountered before. At his old school, he'd been able to walk around and do whatever was comfortable for him. He'd ride his bike to and from campus. He'd play tetherball and four square at recess.

Since the teachers there had known Ben from kindergarten, they were comfortable with his abilities. Teachers like Mrs. Akiyama gave Ben a lot of freedom, and the kids had Ben's back because they knew Ben as one of them. The other staff, from the principal to the school secretary, knew him too. He'd hear a bunch of keys jingling and automatically say, "Hi, Mr. Jim!" That was the custodian.

Ben was just being a normal kid. But none of that was sitting well with the teachers and administrators at the new school. Thankfully, Mrs. Barbara was still working with Ben at his new fourth-grade school, and she had always respected Ben's independence. She was his advocate and my eyes when I couldn't be there. I knew she truly loved him. Though Mrs. Barbara would follow behind him in the building, she never held him or guided him because Ben was able to navigate by himself.

Mrs. Barbara felt it was her duty to help educate the new school's staff about Ben's abilities. She knew that this level of echolocation was extremely rare and that they might not have any idea of what to expect. Some of them were eager to listen and learn. Others, not so much. Mrs. Barbara tried to explain that if Ben had a cane on the playground, he wouldn't be able to play freely. Ben couldn't swing on monkey bars and play other games if he was required to use a cane all the time. If Ben put the cane down, she said it would be fine if it stayed there.

A few times during the school year, we had meetings with

Mrs. Barbara and other school staff to make sure Ben's needs were being served. This boy could be such a character at times. During one meeting, Ben sat sulking a little when someone asked, "Ben, are you finding this boring?"

Ben shot back, "Not as much as that teacher next to my mom."

I just cracked up. Ben could sense that a particular teacher was fidgeting in his chair like he was impatient and wanted to get out of there. Ben could pick up even the most subtle social cues.

Some well-meaning people wanted to keep Ben in a kind of "box." To them, blind people should be treated differently from others, as if they were so delicate they needed to be sheltered from the world. I butted heads with some school administrators over the issue. Convincing them that Ben didn't need to use a cane wasn't an easy sell.

Most blind people who use echolocation use a cane, too, and that's great if it works for them. But Ben thought of his cane as a crutch—not in the literal sense, but as a cop-out. Ben felt that using a cane was teaching himself to be dependent on something besides his own ability. He also believed that using a cane impaired his listening skills because it cluttered his field of sound. Maybe it was partly a pride thing, but since Ben got along just fine without a cane, I wasn't going to insist that he use one. Ben knew how to use a cane, and if someday he wanted to use it, he would.

But if clicking was how Ben learned to survive, I didn't think anything was wrong with that. He wasn't trying to show up anybody or act superior. I just felt sorry that some folks reacted with scorn, though the negative comments were just dirt off Ben's shoulder. His response was always, "Whatever! You don't know me!"

One of Ben's mobility teachers insisted, "You know, when Ben gets older, he'll use a cane."

Well, how did he know that? Let me be real here. That mobility teacher wouldn't have a job if kids like Ben didn't use canes, so it's no wonder he wanted every blind kid to use one.

I was against canes for Ben only because Ben was against them. But I didn't automatically reject any extra resources or help. I talked to Ben once about getting a Seeing Eye dog, but he didn't want one. I left it up to him. I wasn't in Ben's shoes. I have eyes.

There came a point when Mrs. Barbara felt she was spending so much time with Ben that she needed to let other mobility teachers in the district work with him as well. Not every teacher for the visually impaired gets to work with someone like Ben, and she was kind enough to share him.

Unfortunately, when Mrs. Barbara's duties were given to another teacher, he gave Ben a folding cane. Ben immediately put it in his backpack and never planned on using it. Mrs. Barbara always thought that a cane might be beneficial for Ben, especially when he was older and needed to navigate an entirely new place by himself. Still, she understood Ben's perspective and knew his capabilities. In the end, Mrs. Barbara respected Ben's wishes and trusted his instincts. The staff at the new school were not as understanding. Mrs. Barbara called me after school one afternoon, and her voice sounded choked up. Fighting back tears, she said, "Aqua, you're going to need to schedule a meeting with these people. They don't approve of the things that Ben's doing at school, and it's getting tense."

The staff were basically saying, "Ben, you can't get on the monkey bars. You're blind. Ben, you can't ride your bike to school. You're blind. Ben, you can't leave your cane at home. You're blind."

Rather than encouraging him, these people were telling Ben all the things he couldn't do. Mrs. Barbara felt that they were picking on Ben because he was defiant about not using his cane. During the times Ben would hold on to someone as a sighted guide, one of the teachers would say, "Hands off! Nobody touch!" It seemed to me that they only enforced the rule about not touching other kids when Ben used a sighted guide. I wondered if it was a ploy or some kind of punishment because Ben wasn't using a cane.

This wasn't the first time Mrs. Barbara had stood up for kids who weren't fully understood by administrators. She'd taught a student with cerebral palsy and major speech impediments, and she knew that this kid could read despite what everyone else had said.

In my naive mind, I had figured that people would accept Ben for who he was, especially at school. I didn't really understand that they could force a kid to use a cane, even if that cane actually made it tougher for him to get around. So I called the school and said I wanted to schedule a meeting.

On that day, I walked into a conference room at the school. There was a big, long table in the middle with ten or so people around it. I could tell they were taking me seriously. The school principal and vice principal were there. So was Ben's fourth-grade teacher, and a fifth-grade teacher who'd be Ben's instructor the following year. An advocate for the disabled also took a seat, along with a few other staff members. Everyone introduced themselves and explained what their jobs were. Somebody read out the list of rights of the disabled in public schools. It was all very official.

Finally, it was my turn to speak. I stood up from my chair so they'd all have to look up at me. In my firmest voice, this is what I said: "My name is Aquanetta, and I'm Ben's mother. First of all, no one will tell Ben that he cannot ride his bike to school because 'you're blind.' No one is going to tell Ben to get off the monkey bars because 'you're blind.' No one is going to tell him 'hands off, hands off' if another child allows him to use him as a sighted guide. How dare you tell my son what he can't do! From this moment forward, that will not happen again. Not ever. You've all been saying all the things Ben can't do. When are you going to tell him what he *can* do?"

They looked at me like I was crazy, but I'd made my point. That was basically the end of the meeting, and I got a few awkward apologies. We had no more problems after that in fourth grade.

CHAPTER 13

SCHOOL EXPERIMENTS

SOME SCIENTISTS believe that human echolocation is a natural ability for everyone. We can close our eyes, yell a couple of times, and easily tell the difference between a big, empty gymnasium and a small closet. Sighted people don't need to use sound as their primary means for getting around, but blind people can use it to help them make sense of the world.

The only frustrating part for me was when I was unable to describe what Ben was hearing—simply because I couldn't hear as well as he could. I still remember one day when we were in a park, walking by a big, shady tree.

Suddenly Ben stopped. "Hey, you hear that?" he asked.

I tried as hard as I could, even cupping my ear, but I heard nothing.

"Baby, I can't hear it. I'm sorry. I don't even know what you're talking about." And I really did feel badly. I loved using words to paint a picture for Ben of what he was hearing. Sometimes, though, I just couldn't do it.

For the most part, Ben's ability to hear was a great comfort to me. When he was playing in the street with his friends, the faintest sound of a car would make him step back over the curb until he was squarely on the sidewalk. I'd look and see a car turning the corner and think, *Uh-huh, those kids need to be paying attention to Ben.* He'd move out of the way long before anyone else knew a car was coming.

Ben's echolocation wasn't that much different from how certain animals use sound and echoes as an extra set of eyes. Dolphins use high-frequency clicking sounds underwater. They listen for the returning echoes bouncing off objects to picture which predators may be nearby or to find schools of fish that might be their next meal. Some marine biologists think dolphins may use clicking to communicate as well. Bats use a similar system to navigate in the dark, whether they are hunting or trying to disappear from a predator's line of vision.

In the years to come, I'd learn more about echolocation. All I knew, as Ben developed this skill early on, was that it helped him distinguish differences between objects to an astonishing degree. For instance, Ben could tell if a pavement was smooth or rough or if he was standing in front of a plant or a fence.

Ben once said that if he clicked near the surface of water, the echoes he heard sounded just like those made by a person. That makes sense, given that the human body is about 60 percent water.

Neither Ben nor I spent much time thinking about the science behind what he was doing though. I just thought, *Okay, it's echolocation—so what? Don't all blind people do this?* I remember turning the corner on my way home from work one day, only to see Ben riding his bicycle as another boy stood on the rear pegs while holding on to Ben's shoulders. All I could think was, *These kids are crazy.* I passed them up, parked the car, and went into the house.

To me, Ben's sound was a gift from God, something supernatural. I know there was a purpose in my son losing his eyes. Ben would not have been the vessel God intended him to be if he had kept his eyes. I believe his purpose was to be blind, to show others about the possibilities of vision without sight. Ben could see more than most of us, for he was full of faith. It's just like the Bible says in Hebrews 11:1: "Faith is the confidence that what we hope for will actually happen; it gives us assurance about things we cannot see" (NLT).

■ ■ ■

Ben developed an understanding about the circle of life at a young age. He'd ask me why people cried at funerals, since going home to God was the greatest glory of all. Ben even felt this way when his father died. Ben was about ten years old, still a little guy, when we got the news.

Ben and his dad had a decent relationship over the years. Ben's dad was very smart and inventive, qualities that I think he passed down to Ben. His dad also liked to sit quietly and ponder life, just like Ben. They were never super close because his dad lived in Southern California and we lived up north. Ben's dad had a house in Mexico where he would sometimes take Ben and his half-brother. But overall, I raised Ben pretty much on my own, as both his mother and father.

I remember the last phone conversation Ben had with his dad, about a year before Stephen died. Ben was always an excited and happy guy, but his dad was going through some hard times and was depressed when he called us.

Ben picked up the phone and said, "Hi, Dad!" Then his dad started talking in this sad voice, and I could hear Ben's cheeriness start to deflate. Finally Ben handed me the phone after telling Steve, "Oh, okay, why don't you just talk to my mom?"

At the time, Ben and I didn't realize that this would be the last time Ben would talk with his father. I wish that conversation had gone better, but what could I do?

Death didn't seem to trouble Ben. When we went to my grandmother's funeral, Ben asked me, "Mom, why are people crying? If she lived a long, happy life, that's a good thing. Plus, she's with God now, and that's the best thing anyone could ask for."

■ ■ ■

As Ben approached middle school, Mrs. Barbara told me that she thought Ben would benefit from attending a school for the blind, and I was open to the idea. But even among blind kids, Ben was different. For one thing, most people who suffer from a visual handicap aren't fully blind like Ben but have low vision. Many others have additional physical limitations, like cerebral palsy, but Ben did not.

The good part about these schools is that they use technologies and teaching methods for blind kids that go beyond what the public schools have. Some of these special schools take kids skiing and give hands-on lessons for using public transportation. Ben would also get a chance to use touch-typing systems, voice programs on the computer, and other software in their learning labs.

One of Ben's mobility instructors told me about a school for the blind in Fremont, a city in the San Francisco Bay area. By this time Ben was almost a teenager, and I thought attending this school would be good for his development since he had never been around many other blind kids.

Ben spent his seventh-grade year at this school for the blind. He'd stay in Fremont during the week and come home on weekends and holidays. For half the school day, Ben and his classmates would go to a nearby junior high to learn with the regular public school kids. Ben never had trouble making friends, so I figured this would be a fun new adventure for him.

That feeling quickly changed. I knew the school had done a lot of good for so many kids, but we could tell within the first week that it wasn't the best fit for Ben. Everyone at the school had good intentions, but their program was a step backward in terms of Ben's capabilities. The kids were taught to travel together with one student leading in the front, and the others following in various formations so their canes wouldn't hit one another. To Ben, this was like making an Olympic sprinter crawl around a track on all fours. Ben told me he felt like he was losing his clicking skills. Ben would call me, complaining, "Oh, Mom, these kids are blind over here. I'm not like them. They don't let me do nothing!"

Ben had to carry a cane wherever he went, but he used it more as a prop than anything. I reminded Ben that he was lucky to be at a school like this, despite the way he felt. I said he needed to be a good person and do his best to be helpful with the staff and other students. He tried, but I knew he couldn't wait for the year to be over so he could be "Ben" again. The best part of his day was when his class went to the regular public junior high. He felt like he had a lot more in common with those students than the kids at the blind school.

One time when he was home for the weekend, I said, "Honey, I forgot to give you your lunch money for the week."

He said, "That's all right, Mom. The kids at the public school always want to see my eyes, so I take them out for a dollar apiece." He could make fifteen or twenty dollars a day like that!

Overall, the year in Fremont was good. Still, all year long he struggled with the limits and worried about losing his ability to trust his senses. The last straw for Ben was when he brought a rubber ball to school. He always loved to play four square and other playground games, so he didn't think this was a big deal. Wrong. One of the teachers told Ben firmly that he couldn't bring the ball to school because someone might get hurt.

That incident really sunk Ben's spirit. Besides all the follow-the-leader stuff, now he couldn't even play with a ball. Ben begged me to let him leave this school early, but I made him stick it out. I said he needed to finish up the year because transferring in the middle of the school year might not be good for his academics, but I promised he could go back to our neighborhood school for eighth grade.

At least Ben enjoyed being the campus video-game champion. I let him keep his game system at school, and he'd play with the counselors in their dorms. One of the counselors got hooked. He'd call up Ben and say, "Hey, tell me how to get to level 6."

In the end, I'm glad Ben spent his seventh-grade year at this school. He ended up making some good friends, even if he was something like the school instigator. He had those other blind kids practically jumping off the walls, and one girl even broke her arm. I feel bad about that, but what can you do? To enjoy life, you have to take some risks.

■ ■ ■

Ben was back in public school for eighth grade. Academically, he was doing great. He excelled in math. But since he did all his calculations in his head, he didn't show his work. The math teacher gave him a hard time for that, even though he got the right answer before anyone else.

Some of the same old issues flared up again too. Ben had meetings twice a year as part of the Individualized Education Program, or IEP. This program, which includes a team of parents, teachers, and staff, is meant to help students with disabilities reach their educational goals. They'd check Ben's progress and see what other resources he might need.

Ben really hated sitting through those IEP meetings. At this one particular meeting, Ben's mobility instructor started complaining again because Ben wasn't using his cane. Ben was done with this talk.

"Okay, stop right there," he said. "My mom is tired of hearing this, and so am I. I am not using that cane, and you cannot make me."

I tried to reason with the mobility instructor.

"Look, I understand that you've been educated," I said. "You went to school, and you learned how to teach a blind person to use a cane. But here you have this blind kid who walks without using a cane. If you take what you have and what he's learned, and put it all together, you might have something new."

Oh, that teacher got mad! He was already upset with me because I'd shown Ben how to walk to school. This teacher was trying to force Ben to use a cane, but he knew I couldn't care less if Ben used one or not. So I ended up getting written up in Ben's IEP report. The mobility instructor said that I'd refused his services and that walking to school should only be taught by a trained professional.

I just laughed when I read that. I thought, *Who is more trained than a mom? You may be able to teach someone how to use a cane, but I can teach someone independence and confidence. I'm the one living every day with this person. You only see him for little bits of time during the school year.*

At the end of these meetings, I'd always have one thing to say: "Ben is just fine."

■ ■ ■

One Christmas when he was about thirteen, Ben asked for a video camera. That sounds kind of funny, a blind person asking for a camera. But it was obvious by then that Ben could "see" in a miraculous way that only he and God could understand. So I got him a video camera, and he walked around the neighborhood filming people. He interviewed his friends while they were acting silly and running around their lawns, and Ben's recordings were right on. He kept the camera focused on the people he was filming, and he would swing around to the action when he heard other friends laughing or talking.

That same Christmas I bought Ben an electric scooter. He'd wanted one for so long that I finally gave in. I worried at first that the motor might be too loud for him. That could be dangerous if it blocked out the sounds of approaching cars. Ben reassured me that electric scooters weren't loud.

I noticed that Ben didn't go into the street right away with his new toy. First he rode it in the garage for a while, getting a feel for how it worked and hearing what sounds it made.

My uncle came over right after Christmas. As he was chatting in the garage with my aunt, Ben hopped on his scooter. Showing off for them, Ben rode between them, then zoomed down the driveway and into the street. My uncle slapped me lightly on the back of the head—*bam!*

"Girl, what's wrong with you?" he demanded.

"Ow, what did I do? What did I do?" I asked, rubbing my head.

"Fool, you bought this boy a scooter! What kind of mom buys a blind boy a scooter?"

"Well, he said he could ride it. Just look at him go!"

We watched Ben ride in circles around the cul-de-sac like the happiest kid in the world. My uncle's voice softened.

"Yeah, I guess you were right," he said.

"I told you!"

From then on out, you'd find Ben cruising happily around the cul-de-sac as the neighbors looked on in amazement. They'd stand in their driveways for a half hour at a time, watching him turn around the corner, go down the street, and then whiz around the cul-de-sac.

Ben liked to have a little fun with them when riding his scooter. He'd call out, "John, what are you doing over there?" And that neighbor would laugh and ask, "Ben, how do you even know I'm over here? And what are you doing riding a scooter in the first place?"

It didn't matter who came out of their doors or where they were. Ben knew who it was.

■ ■ ■

Building a sense of confidence in Ben meant everything to me. I thanked the Lord that he had always been so strong and enjoyed his childhood to the fullest. This might sound crazy, but Ben was actually excited to be blind. No, that's not a misprint. He told me he thought he had an advantage over sighted people, who often judge others based on appearances. His impressions of other people, he felt, were not tainted by what they looked like.

He knew that our world is obsessed with outward appearances. Ben couldn't fathom the way people were judged by their skin color, the brand names on their clothes, or the kind of cars they drove. Being blind, he felt he was beyond all that. Ben saw right through to the heart of a person. And he knew that the important things about a person are often far below the surface.

Ben would wear the same pair of shoes for over a year. When I told him they were starting to look raggedy, he'd always say, "But they feel good. Why do I need to change them?"

I could buy him Payless shoes, and he'd be content. Clothing trends were the least of Ben's concerns. The shine of diamonds and gold didn't mean anything to him either. Those are great values for a teenager to have. It would be nice if more of them could be like that.

Ben wasn't even self-conscious about the teeth he'd chipped on the playground when he was in elementary school. Other people might've had a dentist fix them, or maybe they'd smile less to hide them. Ben felt that as long as he could still eat, his teeth were just fine.

As a teenager, Ben was confident and comfortable with who he was. "I wouldn't even want to see again," Ben said one day. "With all the corruption in the world, why would I want to see that? The world would be such a better place if people weren't so quick to judge. It would be a better place if none of us could see!"

Whether he was playing a video game or walking to school by himself, Ben thrived on facing challenges he would never have experienced as a sighted person. And then he'd leave those challenges in the dust.

I always reminded Ben, "Nobody's ever going to hand you anything, baby. You have to go get it and make things happen for yourself. I may have eyes, but you have to figure things out for yourself because my world is not your world."

Ben was never the kind of kid who said, "I can't." When he started high school, he had the nerve to tell me one day that he wanted to be emancipated. I just laughed and said, "Boy, what do you know about being emancipated?" That's how confident Ben was in himself. He wasn't even afraid of cooking over a hot stove, though he didn't like the splatter from bacon frying. But Ben made the prettiest eggs and cooked sausages.

He wanted to fry chicken, so I planned to get him a deep fryer someday. I figured we'd fry the chicken on a timer so he'd know exactly when it was ready. I planned to tell him, "Okay, Ben, now season the chicken like this. Put the seasoning in the flour, and then give it a little taste. If it tastes right, then start to roll your chicken pieces in the flour and get ready to cook."

If anything ever happened to me, Ben needed to be able to take care of himself. Nobody on this earth was going to treat him like his mother, so I needed him to be independent and never have to rely on anybody.

We're all capable of doing so much in life, but society's always trying to put limits on us, telling us what we're allowed to do and what we should stay away from. And if you have what society calls a "handicap"—well, forget it. That never made sense to me. I don't care if somebody has no eyes, no arms, and no legs. You don't know what that person can do! Why don't you give him a chance? Let him show you something. Give him the confidence that he can succeed. Sometimes Ben had to learn about his limits the hard way. Other kids had to, and Ben wasn't going to be any different.

In the United States, we should be so much further along than where we are in encouraging the disabled, no matter how old they are or what challenges they face. Some of our teachers and parents are just not empowering our kids. And then you have some parents beating their kids down, telling them what they can't do and putting them in boxes. How can we learn unless we aspire?

CHAPTER 14

TAKING ON THE CHALLENGERS

I TOOK BEN to Take Your Child to Work Day at the DMV one year. Our office was filled with OPEX machines that were high-speed mail sorters. They opened the mail automatically so workers could take out the DMV registration materials inside, or what we called the "pot." On this day, Ben sat next to me, helped run the machine, and then handed me the pots.

Some of my coworkers watched Ben help me and also saw him walk in between all the OPEX machines without bumping into anything. When he tired of that, he hooked up one of his video-game systems to a TV. When Ben started playing, everybody was stunned.

My boss pulled me aside, all excited.

"Aqua, you need to write Oprah!" he exclaimed.

I just laughed it off. But I said, "All right, Daryl, if that's what you think."

"No, you really need to write Oprah. I'm serious."

This went on for about a year. My boss kept asking me, "Have you written Oprah yet? You need to let her know about your boy!"

I finally gave in. There was a section on Oprah's website where you could submit story ideas. I don't remember exactly what I said. I wasn't looking for Ben to become famous or anything. I sent that note mainly so my boss would quit bugging me.

I figured Oprah got tons of requests from people to be on her show, and I didn't think there was any chance we'd get picked. My message to the show was brief, something like, "I have a blind son who taught himself to see using sound. He doesn't use a cane and does the same things as any normal kid."

I hit the "send" button, and that was it. I never received a response, so I didn't think any more about it.

■ ■ ■

As he approached his teen years, Ben loved to do what other boys did, including climbing trees. One Saturday while we were at Tiffany's basketball game, Ben and Isaiah were playing outside the school. At halftime I went to check on them.

A bunch of kids were playing in a huge tree in the middle of this grassy area. Instantly, I knew: Ben was up in that tree! *Oh, Lord*, I prayed, *please don't let Ben fall.* How would I explain that to anybody?

"I hope you can get down!" I shouted to Ben. "Because you know I can't go up there!"

Of course, Ben had to be the kid who was highest in the

tree. He was way up there, like the cat stuck in a tree whose owner has to call the fire department to get him down.

"Watch me, Mom!" Ben yelled back. "I know how to get down!"

And just like it was nothing, Ben slowly started to make his way down the tree. His feet found their way, stepping deliberately onto the branches while he held on to the trunk.

Watching him from a distance, you'd never guess that my boy didn't have eyes. Ben was just like any of the other kids playing out there: laughing, getting dirty, maybe picking up a couple of splinters.

Once Ben plopped his feet back on the ground, he gave me a big wave and laughed.

"Ha ha! I told you that was easy! Next time I'll go higher!"

All I could do was put my hands on my hips and give him a warning. "Boy, you have fun, but don't break your neck up there. We have to fold some clothes and sweep when we get home!"

I laughed and breathed a little sigh of relief. Not only was Ben safe, but there was no stopping him in life. He was free. If Ben could climb a tree like that, Mt. Fuji couldn't be far behind.

Ben sometimes played basketball after school with Mrs. Akiyama's kids. Before they'd start playing, Ben would find his way under the hoop and then jump up to touch the net. After he built that picture in his mind, Ben could shoot baskets just fine.

I enrolled Ben in karate during junior high school. He'd always shown a natural ability for kicking and punching, and he certainly had enough experience fighting with his brothers.

Ben had always had quick hands, and his strong physique was developing even more. Ben's karate teacher, or sensei, really liked having Ben in the class. Every new student starts with a white belt, and Ben graduated from that without much trouble. He learned the basic punches, poses, and kicks. Blocking moves are also a key part of these classes, and Ben swung his arms right in time, well aware of any punches coming his way.

The teacher was astonished at how accurate Ben could be. All it took was one demonstration of a move, and Ben could do it.

He earned a yellow belt, which expands on the beginning techniques of karate. With his sense of space and timing, Ben could easily spar with others, using outside blocks and side-thrust kicks against them. He kept his hips turned a perfect forty-five degrees for a front stance, and he used knife-hand blocks with the bottom edge of his hand to counter any moves by his opponents. Jumping around in his white gi, the uniform for martial arts, Ben looked like a superhero.

As a teenager, Ben joined a wrestling team. Some young blind people, such as Avery Ingram of Oregon, have shown incredible abilities on the wrestling mat. Avery scored twenty victories as a high school wrestler, despite being blind since the age of two.

The rules are usually different for blind wrestlers. They and their opponents must start by touching hands and then maintain some form of contact throughout the match. Ben didn't think this was fair. He wanted to follow the same rules that applied to everyone else when wrestling.

After all, when Ben used his sound, there was no way an opponent could hide easily from him. The way that sounds echo so loudly in the gym really helped him. And once Ben pounced with his strength and quickness, nobody would mistake him for being an easy target. If an opponent thought for a moment about going easy on the blind kid, Ben seized that opportunity and made his challenger regret thinking that way. Ben could still "see" his opponent, whether it was through hearing or even smelling his sweat. He wrestled five matches against sighted opponents and won them all.

■ ■ ■

I haven't mentioned this to many people, but Ben once told me that one of his wrestling coaches took him driving in the empty school parking lot. One of Ben's biggest goals was to get in the driver's seat. To him, it was the ultimate form of independence and rising above his blindness. The reality was there was no way he'd ever get a driver's license. I wouldn't even want to be on the road if Ben was behind the wheel. (Of course, I felt the same way about my sighted kids when they started driving!)

The fact that he couldn't drive—at least legally—didn't stop Ben from thinking of inventions that would make it possible for him to drive someday. He imagined a car in the future that would have sensors in the front and back, with a computerized voice telling him to speed up or slow down, and letting him know if it was clear to change lanes. Come to think of it, Ben's idea wasn't too far removed from Google's driverless car, which uses a built-in mapping system, speed controls, and sensors to gauge its distance from other cars.

Ben didn't get the chance to drive one of those robotic Google cars, but he did take a quick spin. Thank goodness I didn't know about this until after the fact. I loved the idea of Ben testing limits, but I thought him trying to drive was absolutely crazy. However, Ben was one step ahead of me this time.

"Too late, Mom. I already went driving," Ben said after school one day. That's when he told me his coach had let him drive in the school parking lot after everyone else had cleared out. I was floored by this news. "So, Ben, how was it?" I asked, trying not to panic. After all, he was standing in front of me in one piece.

"It was fun! The only thing is I kept hitting the brakes too hard, so the coach kept jerking around in his seat and telling me to ease up on the brakes. But doesn't everyone hit the brakes too hard when they're learning to drive?"

"Ben, you are crazy. Tell me the next time you go driving so I can make sure I'm not on the road."

"Shoot, Mom, next time I go driving, I'm taking you to the store!"

Ben only went driving that once—at least as far as I know—but I'm glad he got to enjoy that experience. From then on, Ben kept thinking about building his own car someday. Ben had the vision of an inventor, and he was really good with his hands. Ben could connect all of our VCRs and DVD players. He's the one I'd always turn to when I needed help hooking up electronics. Don't ask me how he did it—he just did. I suppose if he tried to connect something and it didn't work, he'd just keep going until everything was working like it should.

■ ■ ■

My ultimate goal for Ben was that he would get equal treatment, not special treatment. That applied to our home as well. Ben wasn't going to get any special privileges over his siblings. He was responsible for cleaning the table after dinner. If he'd made a mess in the front room from playing video games or whatever else, that wasn't okay. He had to pick up after himself. Laundry had to be folded, and the trash can needed to be rolled out on Wednesday nights.

Of course, all kids will test you to see what they can get away with. There was a time when Ben and I were in the garage. Just for the fun of it, he was tearing up some paper and throwing the pieces to the ground.

"Don't be throwing a bunch of paper on the floor!" I said. "If you're going to rip up some paper, go throw it in the trash where it belongs. The ground is not a garbage can!"

"Okay, Mom, calm down! I was just messing around."

Ben walked toward the door and left the papers on the ground. I think he sensed I wasn't watching him anymore. Wrong! I was right on top of this. And now he was ripping up even more papers and leaving the pieces on the ground. Oh, that really set me off.

"What did I tell you, Ben? Now get on the floor and pick up every piece of paper that you've dropped! For every piece

I find, that's one less hour of video games for you. Do you hear me?"

Ben knew he was busted. He let out a little frustrated sigh and got down on his hands and knees to gather up the torn paper. I had to teach Ben a firm lesson, but this was hard to watch. I didn't want to see my son on the ground like that. I had to turn my back and go inside while he cleaned up every last piece. At the same time I was thinking, *Who does this kid think he is? There's no way he's going to get away with inconsiderate stuff like this.*

It wouldn't be fair to the rest of the family if I had one set of rules for Ben but held everybody else to a different standard. I wasn't going to walk behind Ben like a maid and pick up every little thing he dropped on the floor. Are you crazy? That boy had to show some responsibility in my house. Like I always told Ben, "Don't make the mess in the first place, and then you won't have to clean it up. Or, if you end up making a mess, clean up behind yourself right then and there."

Whatever we allow our kids to do or not do, that's what we create. I loved Ben dearly, but I wasn't about to raise a mama's boy who couldn't let go of my apron strings.

I was so determined that Ben would be independent that I even had him babysit one time when he was about thirteen. I had to make a quick run to the store, so I asked him to watch over his baby nephew while I was gone. Ben was totally fine with it. All he said was, "Well, you know I'm not about to be changing any diapers." I laughed and reminded him that I wasn't going to be gone that long. I told him that if the baby got grumpy, give him a pacifier.

I know that leaving a baby with a blind kid would rub a lot of people the wrong way. Some folks might even want to throw me in jail for that. But I'll tell you what: Ben could take care of that baby just as well as anyone. He'd sit there all day with that baby if he had to and make sure nothing happened to him. And if by some chance there was an emergency, Ben knew how to call 911. And he could get in touch with me right away or get help from our neighbors if necessary.

People tend to forget that my Ben could see! He just saw differently from the rest of us. I had enough confidence in Ben to leave him in charge of a baby, and he had that same amount of confidence in himself.

CHAPTER 15

REACHING OUT

KAISER PERMANENTE MEDICAL CENTER, SACRAMENTO:
SPRING 2006

Our whole lives changed after a single doctor's appointment.

The afternoon checkup started like any other. It sounds kind of odd, a boy with no eyes needing to see an ophthalmologist. Every few years Ben had to have his eye sockets checked to make sure that they were healthy and that his artificial eyes fit correctly. As Ben waited to see Dr. James Ruben, an ophthalmologist and pediatric eye surgeon, I sat with him in the exam room, reading a magazine. Ben sat across from me tapping away on his Nintendo DS.

Since we hadn't had an appointment with Dr. Ruben in about five years, we barely remembered him, and we quickly realized that he didn't remember us either. When Dr. Ruben finally walked into the exam room, Ben stayed focused on his

Nintendo game. I think he was about to win or something, because he kept looking straight down at the game, pressing the buttons feverishly. Dr. Ruben paused for a second, then walked back out. I figured he needed to make a quick call or something. I heard him go over to the receptionist.

"Where's my patient?" Dr. Ruben asked.

"Doctor, that's your patient right there in the exam room."

Dr. Ruben walked back into our room. He didn't even look at us. Instead, he stepped right between us to see Ben's chart. He flipped through the papers, taking a quick study of Ben's medical history. He turned his head to Ben again, then looked back down at the charts.

I didn't know what was going on. Dr. Ruben went over to Ben and knelt down so he could look up into Ben's face. Ben kept right on playing, like he was in the zone and didn't want to be interrupted. Dr. Ruben then stood up and looked over Ben's shoulder to see if he was actually playing the game or just pushing the buttons randomly. Nope, Ben was indeed playing that game.

"His eyes are enucleated, right?" Dr. Ruben asked me. *Enucleated*, I had learned, was the fancy word for "removed."

"Oh yeah, he's blind. He lost both his eyes before he was three years old," I said.

"Well, how is he playing this video game?"

"Doctor, he plays video games. He rides bikes. He does what all the other kids do."

Dr. Ruben continued to give me a puzzled look. Gesturing to Ben and his DS, he said, "And this is normal for Ben, right?"

Now it was my turn to look surprised. I nodded. The

doctor got really excited. He called for one of the nurses to see Ben. Then he started paging other doctors to come see his incredible patient. Pretty soon we had a little crowd in the exam room hovering over Ben.

"Look at this kid!" Dr. Ruben said to the others. "What do you think? Isn't this amazing?"

Ben started laughing really hard. He didn't get all the fuss.

"Mom, is he serious?" Ben whispered to me. "I'm just playing my game."

"I don't know, Ben. I don't think he's seen anything quite like this. I guess his patients don't play too many video games."

Dr. Ruben believed Ben needed to be on TV, and he wanted to help make that happen.

"We've got to get him on *Oprah* right now!" he said.

"You think so?" I asked, a little surprised. "Ben's been this way ever since I can remember. My kids just like to play video games."

Maybe it wasn't a big deal to me because I'd always thought of Ben like this. All this commotion seemed kind of funny to me, but I went along with it.

Dr. Ruben said the first thing we needed to do was let the local media know about Ben. He arranged to have the hospital's public relations team spread the word, starting with the *Sacramento Bee*, our hometown daily newspaper.

The *Bee* jumped on the story. Cynthia Hubert, one of the paper's veteran reporters, was assigned to cover Ben. She was teamed up with Kevin German, a talented young *Bee* photographer known for his documentary skills and artistic photo portraits. They met with us in a matter of days to start getting the story together. Ben and Kevin hit it off right away. They both had silly personalities and always seemed to be laughing and cracking jokes about each other. It was especially fun to have Kevin around.

Cynthia and Kevin did a fantastic job with the story, which landed on the *Bee*'s front page in May 2006. The story introduced the world to Ben and included wonderful scenes of him swaggering around his school campus and Rollerblading, plus quotes from Dr. Ruben, me, and others.

I didn't expect the response to be so big, but it wasn't long before the TV networks got wind of Ben's abilities and started doing their own stories. I got a call from a producer at the *CBS Evening News* saying they wanted to broadcast a segment about Ben nationally. This would be one of Katie Couric's first broadcasts as an anchor for CBS, and it turned out well.

The CBS reporter, John Blackstone, and a camera crew came to our house and got a lot of great footage. Ben whipped John 5–2 on our foosball table, and they even got caught up in some pillow fights. The segment also showed Ben playing video games with Isaiah. The funny part is that Ben was turned completely away from the TV and facing the couch while playing those video games. All he needed to guide him were the sounds from the game.

Outside, Ben glided around on his Rollerblades for the cameras and took a walk with the reporter. Ben started naming all the objects coming their way: a fire hydrant, cars, trash cans. Ben really blew everyone away when he walked effortlessly around a fallen trash can that blocked the sidewalk. We all loved how this segment turned out.

■ ■ ■

Though the world didn't take note, something else important happened that spring. Our family was back in church, and Ben had dedicated his life completely to the Lord. During eighth grade, he attended a youth service at a local church with one of his friends. After that one service, Ben seemed to know where he was supposed to be, and from then on he was in church every Sunday and sometimes during the week too.

Ben even attended a weekend camp near Lake Tahoe sponsored by the church. He loved camping in the woods. Being in nature seemed to invigorate Ben and give him new sounds and smells to take in. On the camp property there was a big cross at the bottom of a hill where kids could go to pray in solitude or with a group. When some of the kids wanted to go to the cross at night, even though it was deep in the woods, Ben offered to lead the way. "You guys, come over here, this way. Follow me, because there's a bear that way." So they all followed Ben, in the dark and down a hill, and he took them right to the cross.

Ben wanted me to join him in celebrating Christ. He kept telling me, "Mom, you really gotta come to this church." It had been a number of years since I'd been in church, and he kept bugging me about going. My own journey in Christ had gone up and down since the time I was a little girl. I always knew Jesus was there for me, but my dedication to attending church had waned by this point. At the time, I felt closest to God while listening to gospel music, and I always seemed to be shooting up prayers to heaven, asking God to help me or one of my kids.

But Ben was persuasive. I was touched to see Ben so excited after going to that youth service, and I finally told him, "All right, I'll go to church with you. Let's do it."

So in April 2006, I went to my first service in a long while. Even though I hadn't been in prayer or spending a lot of quality time with God, the Lord spoke clearly to me that day. He said, "This is where you're supposed to be. This is where I want you."

It was such a calming feeling, so subtle and sweet, to be back in his arms once again. From that point on, so many good things happened in our lives. The first article in the *Sacramento Bee* came out not long after I attended that service. The beauty of God's love flowed through me, and I was home for good. I've rarely missed a Sunday service since then.

■ ■ ■

I'm grateful that I had gotten closer to God again just before the media's interest in Ben took off. Soon, the daytime talk shows were eager to have Ben as a guest. So we were off for Los Angeles to tape an episode of *The Ellen DeGeneres Show*.

I had no idea what to expect, but we weren't necessarily feeling starstruck. I love everybody, so it doesn't really make a difference who I'm meeting. If I'm meeting you, you're a star to me. But I knew this was a great opportunity to share Ben's story with a huge new audience. You don't get paid to be on these shows, but they take care of your travel and treat you well. We stayed in a nice hotel in Hollywood and ordered room service right away.

Backstage before the show, we had a great time. Everyone

there made us feel very comfortable. Ellen is really hands-on with her guests, and we had fun laughing with her before the taping started. We exchanged a lot of hugs, and she was just so upbeat and funny. She was perky and full of energy, like a hot kernel of popcorn bouncing around the room.

Ben was in a great mood once it was time to film his segment. I was in the audience, and once the music started playing, Ben came dancing onto the stage with a huge smile on his face. The crowd was clapping like nuts and whooping it up. Ben said, "I hear y'all be grooving out here," and then Ellen started dancing with Ben.

Oh, I was so proud of Ben! He left the audience absolutely awestruck when he came onstage. I cracked up watching him boogie like that, thinking, *Man, what a goofy kid!* I loved how Ben could be at ease anytime, anyplace.

Once the interview started, Ben described how he used his sound to get around and said his goals were to become a writer and a video-game designer. I was also interviewed a little from my seat in the audience. I talked about my parenting philosophies as I was raising Ben and how I wanted to surround his life with positivity.

Ellen was so sweet and complimentary the whole time, and she finished by laying a huge surprise on Ben. She presented him with a bunch of gifts, including a Wii video-game system. Ben was super excited about this. The Wii was still about two months away from being released commercially, so he was among the first people to own one. Ben said he'd heard about the Wii on the Internet and was pretty much in video-game heaven. Ellen's gifts also included the game *The*

Legend of Zelda: Twilight Princess, along with three Nintendo DS consoles.

At one point Ellen asked Ben, "How did you get so cool?" And without missing a beat, Ben replied, "I get it from my momma." Now that just about made my heart explode with pride.

■ ■ ■

Everything was happening so fast. Our lives started snowballing as Ben became more of a media figure. One story or TV segment would come out, and we'd immediately hear from another show that wanted to do its own piece on Ben. We'd be home for a few days and then—*snap!*—we'd be off to catch a flight for another appearance. We started getting letters and e-mails from all over the world, too, full of encouragement and stories of how Ben's attitude was an inspiration to others.

People magazine did a feature on Ben. They sent a photographer and reporter to our house, who followed Ben around as he went about his day. Then they gave Ben a chance to swim with dolphins! The magazine took us to SeaWorld in San Diego, where Ben and I met with Bob McMains, who supervises the dolphin program there. Ben was fitted into a wet suit, stepped into a chilly pool, and met Sandy, a five-hundred-pound Atlantic bottlenose dolphin.

Ben sensed Sandy even before she swam all the way to him. Right away Ben said, "Wow, she's huge!"

Sandy then opened her mouth. I learned that some dolphins have up to one hundred teeth, and that looked true of Sandy. Ben picked up on that as well and said, "Man, she has a big ol' mouth."

Bob let Ben touch the dolphin's smooth, almost rubbery body. Sandy then stood up from the water and balanced on her tail, while Ben shook hands with her flippers. For the finale, Ben held on to Sandy's dorsal fin while she took him for a ride around the pool. He really loved it.

Sandy made a lot of noises: squeaks, whistles, and something that sounded like wheezing. And of course, Sandy showed off a lot of clicking. Hearing Sandy's clicks made Ben think about his sound in a whole new way. Ben couldn't believe how fast Sandy could click. It was like a machine gun. It turns out that dolphins can make up to one thousand clicking noises a second.

I couldn't believe that Ben was in the media big leagues. *People* has a circulation of more than three million readers, and for them to run a full feature on Ben was very exciting. It was surreal to be out grocery shopping and see a copy of the magazine at the checkout stand, knowing my son was in there along with all the latest celebrity news and gossip.

Not long after the story ran in *People*, we were flying to Southern California to visit family. While we were getting situated in our seats before takeoff, one of the flight attendants stopped in her tracks right next to us.

"You're the kid in the magazine right here!" she said, pointing to a copy of *People* in our seatback pocket.

"Yeah, that's me," said Ben.

"Would you mind if I made an announcement?"

Ben and I just shrugged our shoulders.

The flight attendant walked to the front of the plane and got on the microphone.

"Attention, everyone. I have a special announcement before we take off," she said. "We have a very special passenger on board today. His name is Ben Underwood, and he's in the latest issue of *People* magazine. He's known as 'the boy who can see with sound,' and it's a fascinating story. I hope you'll give it a read. Ben, can you stand up and wave hello?"

As Ben got out of his seat, everyone turned toward us and started clapping. What a wonderful experience! The Lord was really using Ben as an example to others about how they could make the most of whatever gifts he had given them.

■ ■ ■

Ben's story was destined for the world. I was contacted by Channel 5 in England, which is similar to the Public Broadcasting System (PBS) in the United States. We agreed to let them film an hour-long documentary on Ben. This turned out to be a very involved process. The cameras followed Ben around for almost six weeks. It was like he had his own paparazzi. I don't know how these reality TV stars carry on so easily when cameras are always around to catch their every move. Ben never asked for the spotlight, so all this constant attention caught him a little off guard.

As part of the documentary, Ben was introduced to Daniel Kish, the head of World Access for the Blind, a nonprofit organization in Southern California that teaches blind people to echolocate. Daniel lost his vision at thirteen months from retinoblastoma, the same disease that claimed Ben's eyes, and he's the only blind person to be a certified mobility specialist. Daniel has made it his calling to help other blind people use echolocation through workshops and hands-on training. His organization has already worked with seven thousand blind people around the world.

Daniel and Ben took slightly different approaches when navigating their world. Daniel sometimes uses a cane for extra mobility support, but Ben wouldn't be caught dead with one. As the filming was being done, it became clear to me that even among people who could echolocate, few had mastered this ability like Ben had.

The producers of the documentary also asked a pair of professors at the University of California, Santa Barbara, to study Ben's abilities. In the documentary, you can see the researchers observing Ben walking down a narrow path, noting that he didn't always stay directly in the center but followed the curve of the path perfectly.

In another test, they wanted to determine how small of an object Ben could detect and whether he could pick out the two identical objects among four items they had set on a table. Just by clicking, Ben could identify the two tape dispensers, which were exactly the same. Identifying a coffee mug proved to be a little tougher. He couldn't say what it was, but Ben knew something was definitely there.

Finally, Ben was given a hearing test to determine if his superb echolocation was due to superhuman hearing. When the test showed that his hearing was normal, I wasn't shocked.

I think Ben had been able to develop his brain in such a way that it was acutely sensitive to sound.

The one-hour documentary was called *Extraordinary People: The Boy Who Sees Without Eyes*. It begins by showing Ben in his morning routine of washing his prosthetic eyes and inserting them in his sockets. From there, the documentary captures Ben riding his bike and shooting hoops, with a lot of emphasis on the science behind his sound.

I'm so grateful for all the time Channel 5 spent capturing Ben. The documentary is on YouTube, and it continues to draw viewers from around the world. It's become one of the main ways people learn about Ben's story. Last time I checked, the program had been viewed millions of times on YouTube.

■ ■ ■

It was only a matter of time before Oprah's people called.

I'd almost forgotten about the letter I'd sent to *The Oprah Winfrey Show* several years before. Then, about a month after Ben appeared on *Ellen*, there was a call from Chicago. One of Oprah's producers was on the line, saying she'd seen Ben's story and wanted him to appear on the show. I told her how I'd reached out to Oprah years ago.

"I know. I'm looking at your letter right now," she said.

It all started to make sense in my mind. I thought to myself that having Ben go on *Oprah* didn't happen on my time but on God's time. The first letter I'd written wasn't part of God's plan. Now that the time was right, everything happened when it was meant to.

And it happened fast. Within a few weeks, a camera crew

from *Oprah* came to Sacramento and filmed Ben at school and around our house. The footage would be used for a video to be shown before Ben walked onstage to meet Oprah.

Although Joe and Derius were living on their own by now and Tiffany has always wanted to stay out of the limelight, Isaiah was excited by all the attention Ben was getting and wanted to be a part of it. So I made it a point to include him whenever possible, including our trip to *Oprah*. Soon the three of us packed our bags for the Windy City. It would be a quick trip, just a couple of nights in Chicago, but we were looking forward to it. My cousin and his wife came, too, and we all rode in the limousine that picked us up from the hotel and drove us to the taping.

Ben and I kept a fairly casual attitude. I knew that going on *Oprah* was a big deal, but at the same time I believe that everyone is equal in the eyes of the Lord. Ben also had a down-to-earth way of thinking about celebrities.

Ben and I were going to be seen by a lot of people—the average viewership of *The Oprah Winfrey Show* was more than six million per episode—so I wanted us to be on our best behavior and carry ourselves properly. In a situation like this, you want to represent Christ and who you are.

Ben was featured on a show about "amazing medical breakthroughs." One of the other guests was a woman who'd lost her arm in a motorcycle accident and had it replaced by a bionic arm. Another was an Army reservist who was severely injured by a bomb and had shrapnel in her head. She survived after surgeons removed nearly half of her skull.

We'd signed a contract with Channel 5 that limited some

of Ben's future exposure, so he could only appear on *Oprah* for ten minutes. Compared to the *Ellen* taping, the feel on *Oprah* was more businesslike. I didn't realize they taped multiple episodes on a given day, so the schedule was fairly tight. Oprah didn't have a lot of time to talk, but she was so nice and gracious to us in the green room. She even took pictures with Ben and Isaiah.

Once Ben's segment started, Oprah asked the audience to hold their applause so Ben could use his sound to find his way to the stage. I walked to the couch with Ben, who looked sharp in jeans and a long-sleeved shirt.

I thought it was great when Oprah told Ben, "Hey, Ben, it's Oprah. Welcome to the show. It's nice to see you."

Ben said, "It's nice to see you, too," which was true because you know my boy could see. Then Ben sat down on the couch with a big smile just like he was meant to be there.

This appearance unleashed another flood of letters and e-mails from viewers who loved and admired Ben even though they'd never met him. We were reminded again that Ben was fulfilling a special purpose with his life. The Lord had shown us that it was Ben's time to shine.

By this time, Ben had become a TV veteran. All of his appearances gave me a better understanding of how Ben's sound worked, but it was even more interesting to see how everyone else reacted. As he'd click over a table to demonstrate how he sensed objects and space, everybody would go, "Oooh."

Later I told Ben, "Ah, so that's what you were doing to clean the table." He just laughed. The notoriety was all fine, as long as he did his chores at home when he was supposed to!

Through all this media exposure, we both learned how a little celebrity status changes people's perceptions of you. Ben recognized this right away. Every time the camera crews would come to Ben's school, he'd notice that one girl in particular would always be nearby. Ben said, "Man, she doesn't even talk to me until the TV people come around. Then she's all, 'Hi, Ben!' like she's my friend."

I made a point to tell Ben he needed to stay levelheaded through all the attention, but he already knew that. I reminded Ben that he was a child of the King and that this is what God wanted him to do. I'm glad Ben never saw himself as better than anyone else—or thought that anyone else was better than he was. For all the celebrities Ben met, God was always "the man" to him.

We had a neighbor who usually wanted nothing to do with us—that is, until Ben was on TV. This neighbor seemed really prejudiced toward my family, and he had young daughters who took on that same attitude. They were always rude and disrespectful to the other kids at the bus stop, and their dad was really mean sometimes. Once I saw him giving a bunch of little neighborhood kids a hard time, and I pulled them aside and told them to go tell their parents about what this man was doing.

The Christmas that Ben got his video camera, he was out in the neighborhood filming when that man called the police on Ben, yelling, "Get off my street! Go away!" Ben was just playing with the other kids, and this man was trying to run them off like animals.

I'd just driven from our house when Ben called my cell

phone to tell me what had happened. I turned around and came right back. I parked the car and went marching down to that man's house with a plastic hanger in my hand. I don't know exactly why I was carrying that hanger, but I was so mad that it just made sense. I got to that house and let that man have it.

"I don't know who you think you are!" I yelled. "These kids are just playing, and you have no right to be treating them like this!"

When the man had seen me coming, he had called the police, saying I was threatening him with a tire iron or crowbar. The squad car pulled up as I was yelling at this man while holding a blue hanger. The police started to laugh when they saw that the only thing in my hand was that hanger. I told them to check their reports, that this man had called the police umpteen times on all the kids.

After Ben went on *Oprah*, that neighbor changed his tune and began getting buddy-buddy with Ben. I couldn't believe it. When I saw that man suddenly trying to be all polite, I told him, "I don't even have time for y'all." I'm not the kind of person to say something like that, but I felt he'd been so rude. I thought, *I forgive you, but that doesn't mean I'm going to deal with you now. All of a sudden you want to be Ben's friend just because he was on* Oprah? *Give me a break!*

■ ■ ■

For me, one of the greatest gifts from all the media attention was that it got us back in touch with the Pughs. After my family had moved to Sacramento, the Pughs had moved a few times before settling in Alabama. As a result, we hadn't talked in years. One of Sister Devon's friends e-mailed her a video about a boy who could see with his hearing. Before Sister Devon even hit "play," she knew it was Ben.

After watching the segment, Sister Devon left her number with Cynthia Hubert at the *Sacramento Bee* and asked her to forward it to me. Once I received her number, I called Sister Devon the very same day. As soon as she picked up the phone, we both just cried. Pastor Pugh had to come over and calm her down so she could get the words out. When she caught her breath, she told me she'd wake up some mornings and immediately wonder how the kids and I were doing.

I felt bad for losing touch over those years, especially with someone who'd played such an important role in my family's life. I think sometimes all of us just get too caught up in our everyday lives. That was easy for me since I still had five kids to raise.

Several months later, after Pastor Pugh and Sister Devon had visited with family in Southern California, they came to Sacramento to spend a week with us. During our long-overdue reunion, I told her about all the good things that had happened since I'd moved to Sacramento—how I'd gone back to school, found steady work, and watched Ben and the other children blossom.

Once we reconnected, the Pughs stayed right with me, just like old times. There's nothing more precious than a deep, lasting friendship with someone you know wants the best for you and loves you like a sister.

CHAPTER 16

JAMMIN' WITH STEVIE

BY HIGH SCHOOL Ben had stopped listening to most secular music. He was all about gospel, especially the song "You Are" by Kirk Franklin.

Actually, Ben had been captivated by gospel music from the time he was a toddler. I remember him being just a little bitty guy, right after we'd moved to Sacramento, lying on my lap during church. The praise and worship would be going on, and he'd say to me, "Mom, listen to that drummer! He's got some beat!" Then he'd pick out the various instruments—organ, guitar, bass—by their sounds.

As a teenager, Ben told me that gospel music was good for "flesh control," unlike other forms of music that could drag people to places of sex, violence, and material worship. Ben started writing and recording his own gospel raps in high school. He found a musical mentor in the Sacramento-based producer Ehan "Goldfingaz" McAlister, who'd worked with some of the biggest names in West Coast rap. Now I know that Ehan sometimes puts out stuff with rough language and street talk that I can't recommend, but I will never forget the kindness he showed Ben and his brothers.

Ehan had recorded some sessions for my son Joe, who was an aspiring rapper at this time. That's how Ben met Ehan. Ben also helped Joe work on a CD in 2002. Those two would stay up all night, working out song ideas. Ben was good at helping Joe string together words for the lyrics.

Though Ben had never had any formal musical training, Ehan could see that he had a lot of music inside him, even if his talent was a little raw at first. He'd take some time from Joe's studio sessions to work out tracks with Ben.

On some nights, even during the school week, Ehan would drop off Ben at the house around 2 a.m. I didn't mind because Ben always got to school on time the following morning and didn't complain about being tired. Ehan was bringing out a lot of creativity in Ben, and I wanted to encourage that.

Ehan ran a music studio in a south Sacramento warehouse that was loaded with a thirty-two-channel mixing board, drums, keyboards, a sound booth, and more. Ben would click around the studio to get a feel for the space. He was always eager to learn more about the gear.

Ehan first showed Ben how to use an MPC 2000, a beat machine and workstation that's used by the biggest names in hip-hop. The MPC features four rows of pads, which can each be programmed to trigger different sounds. By tapping those various pads—one might sound like a bass drum, another like a snare—Ben could create some really cool beats.

It didn't take long for Ben to compose some great drum tracks. Ehan would load up the MPC with various sounds, and Ben took it from there. Since Ben saw with sound, his rhythms were always advanced. It's like he was hearing and seeing the beat at the same time. Ben's tracks had a big thump from the bass drum, but the rhythmic patterns he layered on top sounded like a little beat orchestra. Every time he'd go to the studio, Ben would say right away, "Load up the MPC! Lemme get on that!"

Ben also loved to sing. He had developed a deep, strong voice as a teenager but needed some coaching with his pitch in the studio. Ehan helped Ben work out the notes, encouraging him to visualize them. After two or three tries, Ehan said the result was night and day—Ben had it down.

Ben had a thing for wind instruments. He used to carry a little African flute with him and liked synthesizer sounds that replicated other flutes and horns. Ehan taught him how to play various blues scales and other fundamentals on the keyboard. Ben heard these sounds in his head already. It was just a matter of getting them through his fingers and onto the tape.

Ehan would play a chord on the keyboard and have Ben imitate it. Ben would feel out the notes for a few moments until he figured it out. Then he'd hit the chord a few times to show what he'd learned. If Ben had ever taken piano lessons, it would only have been a matter of time before he took his music to a whole new level.

Compared to all the artists that Ehan had worked with before, Ben's musical perception and microphone command ranked him among the best. This might just sound like a proud momma talking, but I think Ehan would tell you the same thing. When several instruments were playing together, Ben could instantly tell if one of them was even slightly off. He'd step into that vocal booth with that booming voice of his and light up the room. He had a naturally aggressive style that sounded even better when blasting out of the speakers.

Ehan concentrated on engineering the tracks, making sure the recording levels and equipment settings were correct, while Ben created a beat on the MPC. Next Ehan would loop it into eight and sixteen bar phrases to set the foundation for the track. Ben would be waiting impatiently to get into the vocal booth and record his raps. He'd tell Ehan, "Okay, I got this done. I'm ready. Let's go in the booth right now."

Ben's lyrics always touched on deep spiritual matters. In one song, Ben sang about rebuking the devil and putting him back in his place, under the ground and beneath Ben's feet. Ehan had learned about music from growing up in church bands and recording gospel artists, but he hadn't heard lyrics quite like these before. At first he thought Ben was rapping about something dark, like a nightmare or some other scary vision. But as he kept listening, Ehan realized that Ben was seeking spiritual truths in the battle between good and evil. This was pretty heavy stuff for a high school kid.

Music was one of Ben's main ways to channel his love for the Lord. One of my favorite songs by Ben was called "J's Up." The track sounded a lot like the Bay Area rap that was popular at the time, with its slow, rumbling beats and crazy synthesizer sounds. Ben produced the whole recording himself: programming the beat, layering some keyboards on top, and then rapping. I really love the lyrics and approach of this song.

The "J" in this song stands for "Jesus." Ben would make a "J" with his thumb and index finger and hold it high, and encourage others to do the same, singing:

J's on the end of my wrist, I hold it high

Throw your J's up high: J's up! . . .
I stay in battle longer with a sword by my side
Bible on my thigh, sword like a samurai.

Ben thought of himself as a spiritual warrior, and a "J" was the sign of his holy gang. While other people were gang-banging in the name of money and violence, Ben wanted to show that he was a spiritual soldier who was willing to lay down his life for the Lord. I admired how Ben could transform the negativities of urban life into powerful metaphors for serving Christ.

■ ■ ■

Ehan provided the creative spark, but Stevie Wonder was the dose of sunshine in Ben's life.

We met Stevie in the spring of 2007 at California State University, Northridge, where the college hosts its annual International Technology and Persons with Disabilities Conference. This event features panel discussions and lectures about the latest technologies for the disabled, such as robotics for young people with visual impairments and Internet resources for teachers. There's also a big trade show that showcases the latest braille readers, software for the handicapped, amplified phones, and wheelchairs. I was fascinated with all the stuff they had on display.

Our trip there was sponsored by Dolphin, a British company that has developed products for the blind, such as computer screen readers and software that converts computer documents into braille. Dolphin was interested in having Ben promote some of their products in the United States. We had heard that Stevie Wonder usually attends this conference, and I thought it would be wonderful to meet him.

It didn't take me long to spot Stevie. He was walking around the exposition hall like everyone else, with an assistant to help guide him. Even though he's a musical legend, Stevie didn't act like he was trying to hold court or needed to stay behind some velvet rope. I talk to everybody, so you know what I did. I just walked right up and introduced myself.

"Hi, Mr. Wonder, my name is Aquanetta," I said. "I have a son who's blind. His name is Ben Underwood. He doesn't have eyes, but he learned to see by using clicking sounds."

Stevie stopped in his tracks. A big smile crossed his face, and he started to get excited. It reminded me of the way Ben's eye doctor reacted when he first watched Ben play video games in the exam room.

"Oh, I want to meet Ben!" said Stevie. "Where is he?"

I didn't realize that Stevie knew about Ben from one of my boy's TV appearances. I laughed to myself, astonished that this musical legend wanted to meet him.

"Ben, get over here," I called out. "It's Stevie Wonder. This man wants to meet you!"

From the moment they met there on the exhibition floor, the two of them were all smiles and laughs, with Stevie telling Ben how he had loved hearing about his story. They seemed to have a lot in common: two African Americans who challenged the usual notions about blindness and also loved the Lord deeply. And despite all those Grammy awards and million-selling songs to his name, Stevie was heartfelt and humble when meeting Ben.

"Stevie, can I get a picture with you and Ben?" I asked him.

"Ooh yeah, I want a picture," said Stevie. "Let's do it!"

We all posed for pictures, and Isaiah even got in them too. What a wonderful moment. In spite of Stevie's kind words, I thought this was just a lucky, one-time encounter. But it turned out that Stevie would be part of Ben's life from then on.

About a month later, Ben and I returned to Southern California. This time, we went to the Beverly Hills Hotel, where Ben was being honored by Looking Beyond, a charity organization that supports and promotes awareness of young people with disabilities. Ben was being presented with their Soaring Spirit Award at a luncheon and silent auction.

These folks do a great job of raising money for their organization. Just one of their fund-raising events raised more than $230,000. I could tell I was in a room with people who were very well-off. You should've seen some of the rings on these ladies' hands! The room was just gorgeous, with a huge chandelier in the center and lovely flower arrangements on all the tables. I was thrilled that Pastor Pugh and Sister Devon could be there with us that day as well.

I made sure Ben dressed properly for the ceremony. He wore a crisp, lime-green shirt with a tie and clear beads on the ends of his braids. I wore a light-green dress, so Ben and I matched. We were both invited to the stage as the crowd clapped and took pictures of us hugging. I spoke a bit about my life with Ben before the boy of the hour was given his award.

But there was a big surprise. Stevie Wonder came onstage to honor Ben, and he helped present Ben with a fancy glass plaque. The crowd loved it! The plaque had a dedication to Ben, and Stevie joked, "Well, if I could see it, I would read it." I laughed and said, "Here, I'll read it for you, Stevie," so that's what I did. Watching Ben and Stevie hug made me so happy, my heart nearly burst. You could really sense the love between those two. With their long braids and big smiles, they almost looked related.

A piano was waiting onstage, and Ben took a seat on the bench next to Stevie. This was such a touching moment for me and everyone there. Stevie played a song that he'd personalized just for Ben, playing that piano so beautifully and singing in that rich, soulful voice that has made him a musical superstar. At the end of the song, the two of them stood up, locked hands, and raised them for the crowd. That was an unforgettable moment for Ben and me.

Stevie sat at our table during the luncheon, and he and Ben exchanged phone numbers. Over the next couple of years, they'd call each other once in a while. I don't know exactly what they talked about, but sometimes they'd be on the phone for hours. They'd truly become friends. I think Stevie saw some of himself in Ben, and I believe they very much understood each other and had similar spiritual goals.

Stevie and I also hit it off really well. I sensed that he was carrying some sadness at the time because his mother, Lula Mae Hardaway, had passed away about a year before. She and Stevie had been very close. Ms. Hardaway had even cowritten a few of Stevie's songs and had instilled a deep sense of pride in him as a child.

On other visits to Southern California, we went to Stevie's church, West Angeles Church of God in Christ in Los Angeles's Crenshaw District. This cathedral is huge and can fit five thousand worshipers in a single service.

When Ben was about fifteen, we visited Stevie's private recording studio. I think that was the coolest thing we got to do with him. The studio is called Wonderland, and there's no better name. It looks like an old Chinese restaurant from the outside, but once we walked into the studio, we felt like we were stepping into a big music store with all the gear a musician could want. One room was dedicated to mixing, and it had state-of-the-art speakers built into the walls. Another room housed Stevie's grand piano and had a drum set next to it. Stevie also used a computer that would complete tasks based on his vocal commands, like "start recording" or "pull up the last track."

Stevie invited our whole family to meet him there and make a little music. Ehan came with us and said he could smell the vintage equipment when he walked inside.

Stevie came in singing, greeting everyone. "Hellloooo, Ben! Hellloooo, Aquaaa! How ya dooooooing?"

Ben was in a silly mood too. He was never starstruck by Stevie, and he playfully busted his chops like he would with any other goofy friend. He went up to Stevie and started poking him in the stomach.

"What's all this?" Ben said to Stevie. "Man, you've been eatin' good!"

Then Stevie turned the focus back on Ben. He started clicking to imitate Ben. "So how do you walk like that? You gotta show me that one." We just howled with laughter.

A jam session was quickly underway. Stevie took his seat at the piano, and Ehan hit the drums. Stevie worked some chords on the keyboard and started to ad-lib.

"Have y'all got any lyrics?" Stevie asked. "You guys got something for this?"

All of the equipment fascinated Ben, and he wanted to touch everything. Ben especially loved playing with Stevie's talk box, an effects unit that allows you to change the sound of a musical instrument using a plastic tube that goes in your mouth. By speaking into the tube or altering the shape of your mouth, you get these funky, almost robotic sounds. Stevie has used a talkbox since the early 1970s, and it remains one of his signature musical tools. Ben got such a kick out of hearing his voice sound all crazy through that talkbox.

Ben kept firing questions, wanting to know how all the gear worked. Stevie was asking Ben questions, too, asking him to name his favorite old-school R & B song. When Ben said, "Man, I don't know y'all's music!" everyone cracked up.

Ben got to play one of Stevie's keyboards, and Stevie played some tracks that he was working on. Stevie even talked about producing a song for Ben. I said, "Y'all need to make me a momma song!" I thought it would be great for them to write a song dedicated to the mothers of the world.

Being around Stevie really sparked Ben's love of music. I thank the Lord for bringing Stevie into our lives. He's more than a celebrity to me. He's a man with a good and genuine soul who's done so much and inspired people around the world with his gifts.

CHAPTER 17

FANS AND FRIENDS

THE WORLDWIDE INTEREST in Ben kept growing. A TV crew from Brazil filmed a news story that was aired in more than two dozen Spanish-speaking countries. Ben was particularly excited when he was booked on a TV show hosted by Mr. Maric, a famous Japanese magician. The show's staff took care of everything: booked our flights, got our passports, and paid all our expenses. Although we'd be gone six days, the show taping would take only one day, so we would have plenty of time to sightsee.

Ben had been fascinated with Japan ever since he got into Japanese anime in junior high. He'd come home, make a snack, do some homework, and then tune into *Avatar: The Last Airbender* or another Japanese show. The high-pitched voices and adventurous story lines in magical lands really stimulated Ben's imagination. He would always tell me,

"Someday I'm going to live in Japan and learn how to design video games and make cartoons. You just watch!"

Soon after we arrived in Tokyo, we went to the top of the Tokyo Tower, which is even taller than the Eiffel Tower in Paris. I described the whole city below us to Ben. I told him I'd never seen so many buildings. Ben was actually kind of restless up there. He wanted to be on the ground, exploring. We ended up shopping at one of the malls, where I bought Ben a kimono. He also fell in love with Kobe beef at one of the fancy restaurants. That's all the boy could talk about over there.

We walked down the crowded streets of Tokyo's Shibuya district, with all the fashionable people rushing to the train station. I liked to describe the things I saw for Ben as we strolled through this sensory overload of a city: "Ben, there's huge buildings all around us, and they're full of billboards with bright lights and video screens. It looks like the place in New York City where the New Year's Eve ball drops every year. Just listen to all those cars honking! I've never seen so many people trying to cross the streets at once. There's even some girls dressed like your anime characters with pigtails and crazy striped socks. It almost feels like we're in a movie, Ben. I don't think I've ever seen a city this busy."

On the day of the taping, Ben blew away the host and the audience. As he came onstage, dramatic music played, like the prelude to some epic battle between good and evil on the Japanese anime series *Naruto*. The whole thing made Ben crack up with laughter. A staff member had placed eight objects on a table onstage and then asked Ben to put his echolocation to work.

Every time Ben located and picked up another object, the audience would go, "Ohhhhhhhh! Aaahhhhh! Eeeeeeeh!" Ben was laughing so hard that it was difficult for him to settle down and click for them.

■ ■ ■

No matter how much Ben was in the media spotlight, I was never interested in capitalizing on his fame. With all the emphasis on celebrity in this culture, I think a lot of people would've seen stars and dollar signs right away. But I never thought about trying to cash in by getting Ben acting lessons or seeing how we could merchandise him somehow. A Ben Underwood video game or action figure? I don't think so.

I was pitched some business opportunities related to Ben. When a movie producer from New York contacted me, I asked him to send me a contract. As I read it, I realized that he wanted Ben's life-story rights and the freedom to change the facts any way he wanted to make a more successful movie. I said, "Give me something else." We went back and forth for a while, and I guess he finally got tired of me. But there was no way I'd sell Ben's life and mine to some producer and let him make us into something we weren't. It wasn't my story or Ben's story to sell; it was God's story.

People would sometimes say, "Ben's famous."

And I'd say, "No he's not. He's just a kid."

I've never been an idol worshiper, and Ben's time in the media wasn't going to change that. The attention was certainly flattering, and I was surprised at how often he'd be recognized in public. We'd be walking down the street or in a store, and someone would stop and say, "Oh, wow . . . you're that kid!"

Ben wasn't affected by the spotlight. He'd hear his friends compare him to Daredevil, the blind comic-book hero who fights for truth and justice using radar-like senses. Ben never thought of his sound as anything remarkable. It's just what he did to get around.

"Mom, people are always acting like I'm Superman or something," he said to me one day after being filmed. "What's wrong with these people?"

"Well, Ben, who else does what you do?" I said.

"I don't get why it's a big deal. I'm just living my life and doing my thing."

"You're just a weirdo," I said with a laugh. "You're just a weirdo clicker."

The truth is, Ben was simply doing something that worked for him. So if I said, "Ben, sweep the floor and take out the trash," he'd go sweep the floor and take out the trash. He wasn't a celebrity in our house; he was just Ben. As much as Ben loved being on TV and sharing his story, clicking to get around was just an everyday thing, like brushing his teeth.

I'd remind Ben that yes, he was just a normal kid. But at the same time, he could do something that seemed magical to others. I'd tell him, "Your gift is for the benefit of other people, to show them that with faith in God, anything is possible."

CHAPTER 18

VISION BEYOND SIGHT

I FINALLY REALIZED what the Lord had meant when he spoke to me in 1994, saying that Ben's blindness "wasn't for me." I understood that Ben was blessed with a gift to inspire people, to show that nothing is impossible in life when you have faith and believe. Ben lived to inspire the millions of people who had seen him and to show the world God's glory.

Even though Ben was barely a teenager, he focused on learning all he could about the Lord, as well as loving everyone and spreading God's Word. What I'd seen as spiritual sparks throughout Ben's childhood had blossomed into full dedication to Christ. Once Ben started high school, he was a bold witness who tried to convert just about everyone he knew. He'd remind his older brothers, Joe and Derius, that they "needed to get right with God." Ben would chastise Isaiah for cussing and insist that he come to church.

There were times when he literally preached to his class-mates. One day on his way home from school, he heard two girls about to have a fight. He stepped in between them and demanded, "What are you girls fighting about?" Then he started telling them what the Bible says about kindness and patience. Other kids stopped to listen. A police car cruising by saw the crowd and stopped. When the officers figured out what was happening, they stayed and listened too.

One of the teachers at Ben's high school started to call him "Prophet." Every time the teacher would run into Ben before school or in the halls, he'd say, "Good morning, Prophet. What's the good word for the day?" Ben would answer right back with some Scripture that he'd memorized.

I wanted to get Ben a good Bible since that's where his whole life seemed to be centered now. I thought about buy-ing him a Bible in braille, but those books are humongous. They can cost hundreds of dollars, and the full set sometimes weighs more than sixty pounds. Instead, I bought Ben a Bible on a set of CDs. He would listen to the Scriptures over and over until he had them memorized. Some days it seemed as if the earbuds were glued to his ears.

Ben's ultimate goal was to memorize the Bible, word for word, from beginning to end. His first goal was to memo-rize the entire book of Matthew, the first book of the New Testament. It was a great starting point for Ben since this Gospel covers the life of Jesus and illustrates some of his mir-acles, including restoring sight to two blind men in Matthew 9. Naturally, this was one of the stories Ben was most inter-ested in.

Many times I'd come home and find Ben lying back in his bed, deep in thought. It was a form of meditation and prayer that he called "dozing." It was something he always did alone. Watching him, it would have been easy to assume that he was just resting by withdrawing from the world. Yet I believe this was the time when he allowed God to strengthen his soul. I heard him say several times, "My flesh may want to give up, but my spirit says, 'Come on, Ben, we're going to get through this.'"

Spirituality was a deeply personal thing to Ben, an inward journey that required quiet time. He certainly loved the energy of a good church service and being surrounded by others celebrating their faith, but he really cherished times of solitary reflection too. He'd listen to those Scriptures on his iPod and ponder them for hours.

Ben described himself as a "king in Christ." "A king has his soldiers," Ben said one day. "Those soldiers can sometimes get angry with their king if he doesn't treat them with respect. You should be a king who serves others. A king has a lot of responsibilities, not just to sit on the throne and give orders. A good king touches people. Serving others is always better than serving yourself."

■ ■ ■

Ben's love for the Lord carried over into his love for others. His nature was to help others through trying times or to laugh along with them in joyful moments. People of all ages reached out to Ben for his unique wisdom and kindness.

Ben dreamed that someday he'd buy a big piece of land

and let people live on it when they needed to get their lives straight. He imagined it would be a place for homeless people or anyone else who was struggling and needed some support.

Once Ben reached junior high, our home phone had basically turned into "Ben's hotline." Ben had such a positive outlook and was so outgoing that the phone rang all the time with friends wanting to talk with Ben about a personal crisis or simply have him keep them company. Many nights I'd have to tell him to hang up and get to bed.

One friend who called Ben regularly was in remission from leukemia. She and her family had gone through a scary episode, and their spirits were always low. Ben's the one she counted on to get her smiling again. I'd hear Ben tell this girl, "Hey now. You can't be calling me if you're going to be all sad and stuff. You've got to talk happy if you're going to talk to me!"

This girl told me later how much Ben's conversations meant to her. He was the one person who gave her something to live for when everybody else was planning for the worst. To hear a teenager say that really touched my heart. Whatever Ben was telling these kids, I wanted him to continue doing that, because it was part of his calling. Two of Ben's greatest gifts were his abilities to show love and to maintain a positive attitude no matter what life threw at him. God gives all of us gifts like these, but they're not for us to hold on to. They're for us to share and give back. That's where love comes from.

Ben always had the deepest love for his siblings, and he sometimes counseled them too. Sure, kids are going to fight and get on one another's nerves at times, but ultimately Ben was close and protective with his family. He and Tiffany were especially tight. I always thought they were similar in spirit, both good-natured and wise.

When Tiffany left home to attend Delta College in nearby Stockton, the transition was tough for her. Not long after, she called the house feeling overwhelmed and wanted to talk to me. I wasn't around, but Ben was.

"Ben, I just can't do it anymore," Tiffany said.

"You can't let other people dictate how things are going to go for you," Ben told her. "I know that things get rough, but you have what it takes to make it through. We're all here for you. Go do your thing."

And so she did. In fact, Tiffany worked hard at school. She earned her associate's degree and eventually her bachelor's degree in accounting.

■ ■ ■

I noticed that Ben was getting a lot of phone calls from a girl named Anndrya. When Ben first went blind, I was afraid that girls might never like him. The truth is, by high school, girls were very drawn to Ben's outgoing personality and wise soul. Ben was also growing into a handsome young man, with a lean yet muscular physique and some swagger in his walk. His huge smile was impossible to resist.

It seemed like Ben was talking about some new girl every week, but I could tell Anndrya was special to him. She was a cute Latina girl with a kind spirit, and she loved to joke around with Ben. Those two really connected.

When Anndrya met Ben in their ninth-grade science

class, she didn't realize he was blind until another classmate told her. Actually, she found Ben kind of annoying at first. They sat next to each other and were assigned as partners for class experiments. Ben would try to run the show. He'd tell Anndrya that she was doing the experiment wrong, and Anndrya would get frustrated and say, "Look, I'm just trying to help you!"

Ben's laugh and positive attitude ultimately won her over. Soon, Ben was walking with Anndrya in the hallways between classes, resting his hand on her shoulder so she could help guide him around campus. They started walking to school together and hanging out after school as well. Ben would sometimes tease her about his "girlfriends." Anndrya told me later that made her mad.

They'd spend hours on the phone together. Anndrya would sometimes complain about her parents, but Ben would try to put everything in perspective. I'd hear him say, "I know you get irritated with your mom. Just calm down. Your mom's trying to point you in the right direction because she cares about you. Some parents out there don't care about their kids. I know she can get annoying. But be thankful that you have a mom who only wants the best for you."

Anndrya ended up confiding in Ben about some very personal family issues. I don't know the full gist of it, but something in the background had been tearing at her family for a long time. She knew Ben could be trusted, that he was willing to spend hours on the phone with her if she really needed to talk.

"You can't always dwell on the negative," Ben told her. "Once those bad thoughts get into your head, you have to immediately fight them back with a positive thought. It's like training your mind to always go in a positive direction. Life is beautiful, 'Drya, and there's so much to do. It's all a matter of what you're willing to do with it. And you know I've got your back. You are my best friend, and I love you."

Anndrya hadn't known a high school boy quite like this who gave such good advice and stood so strong for her when it seemed like everything else was going wrong. It's no wonder their friendship blossomed and they became high school sweethearts.

Those two spent a lot of time together. She loved baking him cookies and cakes, and he loved visiting her family. They often grabbed a bite at Taco Bell after school. Burritos, after all, were one of Ben's favorite foods.

Anndrya told me about something unexplainable that happened one day at Taco Bell. The hot sauce packets there have a bunch of little sayings on them, like "Is it me, or is it hot in here?" and "Where have you been all my life?"

After picking up their order, Ben and Anndrya carried their trays of food to a booth near the register. Before sitting down, Anndrya went back to the counter to ask for some sour cream.

As soon as she returned and sat down across from Ben, he handed her one of the hot sauce packets.

"Uh, hello, I don't like Fire Sauce," Anndrya told Ben. "You know that's too hot for me."

"No, read the packet," said Ben.

Anndrya looked at the packet in her palm. The saying read, "Will you marry me?"

"Do you know what it says?" Anndrya asked.

"Yes, I do. It says, 'Will you marry me?'"

"What? Who told you that?"

"Nobody told me."

Anndrya looked around. They were the only two eating in the restaurant.

"C'mon, Ben, you're blind. How do you know what it says?"

"The same way you know. I read it," Ben said with a laugh. "I already told you I can see! Keep this hot sauce. If anyone ever tells you I can't see, just show them this packet."

Anndrya slid the hot sauce packet in her pocket. It's something she treasures to this day.

How does a blind teenage boy—without eyeballs, no less—see at random times like this? I can't explain it, and Ben didn't even try. While this didn't happen often, it happened enough that I wondered what was going on. And then I'd think of the passage that says, "Now all glory to God, who is able, through his mighty power at work within us, to accomplish infinitely more than we might ask or think" (Ephesians 3:20, NLT).

That satisfied my questions because I know God's Word cannot lie. The thing we have to ask ourselves is, Do we believe?

■ ■ ■

Ben was definitely wired differently from other kids. He used to express some fairly deep thoughts for a kid his age, sometimes speaking in allegories. I remember how he'd talk about people as blades of grass:

"Blades of grass grow in groups. You will not find just one piece of grass growing on its own. Weeds grow together, and plants grow together. That plant has to have support from other places: from worms, sunlight, water, and other plants around it. They all share some kind of connection. It's the same thing with hair. You don't grow just one long strand of hair.

"If there were just one blade of grass, that piece of grass would die. With a single piece of hair, that would break off from you just moving around.

"The only way you can bring peace to yourself is by bringing peace to others. Serving others is better than serving only yourself."

Ben could also see right into the heart of a person. I remember riding on an airport shuttle with him, and I sensed he felt uncomfortable because of the way he was shifting around in the seat.

Ben whispered in my ear, "Oh, Mom, that man across from us is really evil."

I looked at that man, and something indeed seemed sinister about him. He scowled at us and arched his dark, bushy eyebrows. It almost looked like he was growling. If you put some horns on this man's head, he'd fit the description of a demon.

"That man does look really evil," I whispered to Ben. "Just leave him alone."

For the rest of our shuttle ride, I couldn't look at that man because he looked so scary. Even though Ben didn't have eyes, he didn't want to face that way either. Go figure that one.

On the other hand, Ben could sometimes sense beauty and purity in people just by being in their presence.

We were visiting the California State Fair one summer, not long after Ben had been featured on the local TV news. A lady came up and wanted to shake his hand, saying she enjoyed watching him on TV and how fun it was to meet him. She was a beautiful woman with light caramel–colored skin, high cheekbones, and big, friendly eyes. I thought she looked like a model.

The conversation didn't last long, just enough to exchange a handshake and a few pleasantries. She still left quite the impression on Ben.

"Oh, Mom, she was pretty," Ben said, as the woman walked away.

"Yes, she sure was. How did you know that?"

"I already told you I can see! I could see her heart."

"And what did you see in her heart?" I asked.

"Kindness. Happiness. I could see how pretty she was both on the outside and inside."

I'd sometimes get caught off guard by Ben's perceptive skills. One day when we were driving home together, I was feeling a little frustrated with him. He'd been slacking a bit on his chores and butting heads with Isaiah a lot—just typical family stuff. We stopped at a light, and I turned to Ben to begin chewing him out. Ben beat me to the punch.

"Mom, why are you looking at me like that?" he said.

I was so stunned I almost swallowed my gum.

"Boy! How do you know I'm looking at you and *how* I'm looking you?"

Ben started to laugh, and so did I.

"Ben, you know you're a little weirdo, right?"

"You're the weird one, Mom. I keep telling you I can see!"

I would love to say that I understood exactly what Ben meant; all I know is that when he was in tune with the Spirit of God, he seemed to have a supernatural ability to see. Ben was a very wise soul, but he was such a jokester by nature too. I liked that he had some balance in his personality.

A lot of kids would naturally be curious about Ben's blindness and ask him to take out his prosthetic eyes. He thought it was funny when kids were freaked out by this. One time Ben and his sister went to a roller-skating rink, and some kids asked Ben to take out his eyes. So he started charging them, just like he "earned" his lunch money in seventh grade. In the end, he made about ten dollars and laughed all the way to the bank.

CHAPTER 19

A CHANGE OF PLANS

Ben kept squeezing the sinus area above his nose. He told me his head hurt too. We were on the flight back from Japan after his appearance on a second TV show there. We'd done a lot of flying by this point, and I knew the cabin pressure could sometimes make our ears pop or cause our heads to feel a little funny. I figured all Ben needed was a dose of aspirin or some allergy medicine.

It wasn't like Ben to complain. He told me before the trip that his head was bothering him a bit, but I didn't think much of it. Now Ben asked me for a tissue and blew his nose. When I saw spots of dark-red blood dotting the tissue, I got concerned. There was also some kind of weird-looking chunky stuff mixed with the blood. I didn't want to alarm Ben, so I tried to keep my nerves together and hoped it would pass. We could get Ben checked by a doctor once we landed back in Sacramento if the bloodiness didn't clear up. I figured Ben had picked up a nasty sinus infection or something.

I felt a little comforted that Ben wasn't overly bothered by his headache. He mostly kept his earbuds in and tried to sleep for the nine hours or so until we got back home. We'd been on the go since we arrived in Japan, and the sixteen-hour time difference had rocked our sleep schedules. More than anything, we were trying to catch up on some rest.

This was our second trip to Japan in a year, and we'd had just as much fun this time as we'd had on our first trip. The flight from Sacramento had been wonderful. I savored all the hours I had to read, pray, and meditate on God's Word. I rarely had free time, so I'd felt so blessed to have all that time to myself, as well as the knowledge that Ben would share his story with another set of TV viewers in Japan.

On this trip, Ben had appeared on a talk show as part of a segment on people with superhuman senses. Another guest was an African Bushman hunter who used his extraordinary eyesight to see prey that was more than a mile away. I'd never seen anything like it.

For all the good times we had in Japan, something unsettling happened one day. While sightseeing and shopping around Tokyo, Ben and I came across a Shinto shrine. These sacred structures are all over Japan and are said to house the spiritual forces of the Shinto faith. The shrine's elaborate architecture and curved roof made me curious. I wanted to take a closer look and go inside, but Ben refused. He didn't like the feeling he was getting from this shrine. While inside, I randomly selected one of the *o-mikuji*, or fortunes, written on a scroll. Then I asked our tour guide to translate it for me. Mine read, "*Dai-kyō*," or "great curse." I was so spooked that I had to get right out of there. I didn't mention anything to Ben, but I realized that he really did have an unusual sensitivity to the spiritual realm—and that, in some ways, I could learn from him.

■ ■ ■

I knew Ben needed to see a doctor as soon as possible. He was blowing his nose even more as we got closer to home, and the bloodiness wasn't going away. I tried to keep our spirits up and our minds occupied. Like all the other times we'd flown back into Sacramento, I described to Ben how our city looked as our plane got closer to the airport. I wondered what it must have looked like inside Ben's head.

"Ben, I can see the dome of the capitol in the distance. And there's the Sacramento River next to all these plots of farmland that look like huge green squares. The day is sunny and clear—perfect for Mother's Day weekend. I see a lot of boats on the river. What great weather for returning home."

Ben's nosebleed started again as the plane prepared to touch down. He used some more tissues but stayed focused on his Game Boy.

"Is your head feeling any better?" I asked, looking for reassurance.

"Yeah, Mom, I'm doing okay. Now stop asking me. I'm about to get to level 5 on this game."

"Boy, we're about to land, so you need to be putting away that Game Boy as it is. We can go see a doctor tomorrow after church. They're going to have a special Mother's Day service, and it should be good."

■ ■ ■

The next morning was like any other Sunday at our house. I was up early getting ready for church, and everyone else in the house was still asleep.

"Y'all get up," I finally called. "Ben! Isaiah! It's 9:30. I'm not going to let y'all make us late for church!"

"I'm already up, Mom," said Ben.

Ben's voice sounded stuffed up, and over a quick breakfast he mostly kept to himself. Something wasn't right. Usually he'd be cracking jokes or pestering Isaiah. I checked in with him again.

"Ben, how are you feeling today? Remember, we have to see the doctor later so they can figure out what's going on."

"I'm going to be fine, Mom. My head still hurts a little. But it's not as bad as yesterday."

My boy had earned the nickname "hyphy Ben" at church since he danced with wild energy during services, like the way people move in crazy hip-hop videos. This Mother's Day service was definitely meant to get people out of their seats to celebrate the gift of motherhood. With the joyful music filling our ears and hearts, all us mothers held our hands high in praise and thanked the Lord for blessing us with our children.

Ben's mind was somewhere else. He hardly danced at all.

Instead of acting like "hyphy Ben," he sat quietly in deep thought—and that just wasn't like Ben in church. I focused on praying for my family and rejoiced in all the miracles we'd seen, knowing that the Lord's strength had brought me to this wonderful place.

"How's it going?" I whispered to Ben before the sermon started.

"I'm just a little sleepy. I think I'm still tired from Japan. Don't worry, I'm cool."

After church, I was relieved to see Ben acting more like his usual self. He was laughing with his buddy Angela, a young lady who was originally from Africa. They were talking about *ugali*, an African bread that's eaten with African greens. It's usually rolled into a ball with your right hand and then dipped into vegetable or meat stews.

"Mom, I want to go with Angela to eat some African greens and *ugali*," Ben said with a toothy smile.

"Boy, we're supposed to go see a doctor in a little while! Don't you want to know why your head's hurting?"

"I won't be gone long. I'll just call you when I'm ready to be picked up, and then we'll go to the doctor."

While Ben was off and grubbing down on that *ugali*, I went home with Isaiah to have lunch. I was still feeling jet-lagged from the trip, so I whipped up an easy meal: fat hamburgers that any twelve-year-old boy would love to eat.

Our house felt unusually quiet with just Isaiah and me. My other sons weren't able to make it for a visit, but they both called to wish me a happy Mother's Day in their own way. Joe told me how much he loved me and added, "Thank you for being my mom." Derius, the quiet one, simply said, "Hi, Mom. I love you—just called to say hi." My daughter, Tiffany, soon pulled up to the house. Whenever she wasn't playing basketball for Delta College over the weekend, she made the trip home to be with us.

All of my kids make me feel like a special mom. I'd done my best to raise them to be successful adults and true assets to society. My goal for them always remained the same: at the age of eighteen, they would move out, be well-equipped to take care of themselves, and visit whenever we had family get-togethers. Whether or not that goal has always come true, they've all blessed me with the joy of being their mother.

Ben called to say that I didn't need to pick him up since Angela could give him a ride home. Good. I could relax a little more before taking Ben to the doctor. He'd been gone for three hours, and I could hear in his chirpy voice that he'd had a good time.

When they arrived at the house, Angela said that Ben had talked on the phone to James, her boyfriend who lived in Oakland. Ben was getting goofy with him and saying stuff like, "You better watch out, James! You know I'm going to take your girlfriend from you!"

That was just Ben's humor. Angela made it sound like Ben and James had become fast friends. Ben kept laughing and saying that he wanted to see James next time we went to Oakland. After worrying so much about headaches and bloody noses, my Mother's Day was ending on a happy note.

But we still had to get to the hospital. Since it was Sunday and the doctor's offices were closed, that was our quickest option for finding out what was going on with Ben.

■ ■ ■

I wasn't in a hurry to get to the emergency room. I'd been there enough times to know that we'd probably be in for a long night by the time we saw a doctor. I told the receptionist that Ben was complaining of a headache and pressure in the front part of his head. I also mentioned Ben's battle as a child with bilateral retinoblastoma and explained why he didn't have eyes. To my surprise, that's all it took for us to meet straightaway with a doctor. They said the paperwork could wait until later and ushered us right back into an exam room.

The emergency room doctor didn't waste much time either. Instead of any small talk or questions about what pain medications I'd been giving Ben, he immediately ordered a CAT scan to see what was going on inside Ben's head.

"Based on what Ben's saying, what do you think it could be?" I asked.

"Well, it's hard to say," he said. "It could be as simple as a bad sinus infection. Seeing Ben's medical history, I just want to rule out anything more serious. We'll have to see if the X-ray tells us anything and take it from there."

While Ben was getting set up for his CAT scan, I focused on staying positive. On this Mother's Day evening, it was just me and a bunch of magazines in the radiology department.

In my head, I listened to the voices of my children wishing me a happy Mother's Day. I pictured Ben getting so excited to eat that *ugali* and spend good times with his friend. I thought about my softball coaching season kicking in now that spring was here, and about how we should start planning a little summer family vacation. I gave thanks for all the traveling we'd done and for the many people around the world who had been inspired by Ben's abilities. I prayed that everything would be all right and that the Lord would watch over Ben.

After about an hour, the CAT scan was complete, and Ben and I returned to the exam room. When the doctor finally came in, he told us he had the test results and wanted to discuss the next course of action. I knew by the way the doctor looked at me that something was wrong. That nervous feeling I'd had way back when I was pregnant with Ben swept over me again. I felt my blood pressure shooting through the roof and my palms turning moist.

"Unfortunately, I have some bad news," said the doctor. "We're not exactly sure what the problem is. Judging by the X-ray, it looks like Ben's brain is hemorrhaging."

I closed my eyes, wanting to scream, but I was too stunned to do anything except sit there in silence. My soul had been shattered enough times in my life. All I could think was, *Oh, Lord, here we go again.*

"Doctor, what do you mean he's hemorrhaging?" I said, my voice cracking in frustration. "Are there tumors in his head again? Just what is going on here?"

"We don't have all the answers yet, but we need to move quickly," he said. "I've already alerted the hospital in Oakland that Ben needs to be admitted right away for surgery. We're going to have an ambulance take him there immediately."

I closed my eyes and clenched my hands into tight fists.

"I'm sorry, Aqua," he said, placing his hand on my arm. "I was hoping for better results. I'm glad we caught this when we did."

The whole situation was like an ugly but all-too-familiar dream: hospitals, gut-wrenching test results, emergency surgery. We were in for another battle.

As I was making a mental checklist of everything I needed to do, I noticed Ben dialing his phone to call a friend. I couldn't believe what I heard next.

"Check this out. I'm in the hospital, and my brain's leaking!"

"Boy, stop saying that!" I yelled. "That sounds crazy!"

"Mom, why are you trippin'?" said Ben, hanging up abruptly.

"The doctors always told us your cancer could come back, and this might be it. They figured it wouldn't happen until you were older, but they couldn't be sure."

"Well, if that's the case, so be it," said Ben.

"No, Ben, you don't get it! This is no time for acting cool. You need to quit messing around and start listening."

"Mom, we need to listen to God," Ben said calmly. "Don't you remember that the Lord has a plan for each one of us? If my plan is to get cancer again, then that's what it is. It's selfish for us to try and get in the way of God's work."

"Baby, you could die!" I blurted out.

"Well, Mom," Ben said, "then you just be ready to meet me there."

I took a deep breath and looked at my Ben. He was a young man now, with his strong hands and chiseled face. My soul felt splintered into a million pieces, but when Ben said, "then that's what it is," a calm came over me. Ben was prepared for whatever was next, and we needed to let the Lord guide us. Ben was right. I would have to be ready too.

"All right," I said. "Let's do this."

CHAPTER 20

IN GOD'S HANDS

THE ROAD TO SURGERY was more like a race. Within hours of the CAT scan, he was taken by ambulance to Oakland for treatment by pediatric brain surgeons. The hardest part was not knowing what we were dealing with. It appeared that Ben's brain was hemorrhaging, but the doctors would need to do more tests to discover exactly what was wrong.

I didn't know how this all fit into God's plan for us. The Lord had spoken to my heart when Ben was two, saying he would live and not die. I'd memorized the healing Scriptures, like Psalm 91, but I couldn't figure out why we had to go through this again. I had lost my dad to cancer when I was fourteen. The thought of losing Ben now was devastating. All I could do was hold on to God's promises. God would provide. Jesus had died on the cross. He knew all about suffering. I prayed, asking God for strength. *Lord, as I go through this, I'm trusting in you.* I thought God might speak to me again like he did when Ben was a toddler, but he didn't.

I was feeling especially shaken this time. Ben's senses were the key to his survival. He needed sharp hearing so he could see with echolocation. He also used smell to help process his surroundings. Sometimes he'd open a door and say, "I smell some feet! Who's in the room with you?" This next procedure might wipe away Ben's sense of smell. I was also worried that brain surgery could affect his hearing. If that happened, Ben would be back to square one.

I rushed home to pack some clothes and get my affairs in order while Ben was on his way to the Bay Area. I didn't know how long I might be away. I called one of my aunts who lived near Oakland to explain what was going on. And of course, I had to call my pastors. My brain felt dizzy with emotions and anticipation as I tried to comprehend the seriousness of the situation. My body was on autopilot as I packed a small suitcase.

I wanted to know what was going through Ben's mind. Was he feeling lonely or scared since I wasn't in the ambulance with him? Was he really serious about me being ready to meet him in heaven? Did he truly understand what he was facing right now?

I couldn't get to Oakland fast enough. It turned out that I reached the hospital before Ben did. The ambulance took a different route and ended up stuck in traffic. When Ben finally showed up about forty-five minutes later, I was thoroughly stunned, but in a good way. He was laughing and acting silly with the ambulance driver, dealing with everything and living in the moment like he always did.

The doctors knew about Ben's childhood cancer and were fairly certain it had come back. But to be sure, they put Ben through a bunch of procedures and exams, checking his whole body for more tumors. We arrived on a Sunday and stayed until Wednesday as they finished all the tests.

Monday morning at school, word spread that something had happened to Ben. He and Anndrya were in the same first-period class, and their teacher knew they were close. As Anndrya slipped into her seat in the front row, she heard him mention something about Ben to her. When she gave him a puzzled look, he told her he had an announcement to make.

As class began, the teacher explained to the students that it appeared that Ben's cancer may have returned and that he was in the hospital in Oakland. His classmates reacted with disbelief, but nobody was more upset than Anndrya. Shaken and crying, Anndrya called her mom, asked to be picked up early from school, and demanded to see Ben right away.

■ ■ ■

The MRI revealed a tumor in Ben's sinus cavity the size of a small lemon. The doctors said they'd have to operate to see exactly what kind of tumor it was. The plan was for us to go back home to Sacramento that Wednesday night and return to Oakland the following Monday. When we went back, doctors used that whole day to run another MRI. Ben wouldn't have his operation until the next day.

Ben's new friend James, Angela's boyfriend, learned about

the surgery. Since James lived nearby in Oakland, he came to the hospital that Monday, the day of Ben's presurgery procedures. This was the first time the two of them met face-to-face. James had called his pastors, and they were already praying for Ben. A group from James's church was planning to stay with me in the hospital and pray while Ben was in surgery.

I'd been praying plenty. I kept hearing the Lord tell me, "Go alone, go alone." I didn't understand what that meant, so I called Sister Devon to get her insight. She said, "That's right. God wants you to go to this surgery alone."

This surgery was going to take quite a few hours, and I'd go nuts just pacing around the waiting room. I told James that I'd love to be in praise and worship somewhere instead. He smiled and told me his church was planning a praise and worship service the following morning. That was perfect for me. James called his pastor to say I was coming to their church on Tuesday.

■■■

On the morning of the surgery, May 22, 2007, Ben sat in the prep room wearing his hospital gown. He quietly prayed to himself, with each tick of the clock bringing him closer to being taken into surgery.

A doctor came in and somberly delivered another heavy dose of news. The latest scan showed that Ben's tumor had grown by 50 percent in just seven days and was probably still growing. The doctors weren't sure what they were dealing with anymore.

Ben and I tried to let this all sink in. This tumor was far more aggressive than we'd imagined. When we finally got word that the surgeons were ready to begin, I knew I needed some strength from the Lord. I wanted to cover this whole situation with the blood of Jesus and pray for the medical team. I asked the doctor if we could pray with him. He agreed.

"Ben, get up," I said. "Let's pray."

We formed a circle with the doctor and nurse in the room and joined hands.

I began praying. "Lord, please take care of my baby. Cover this room with your Spirit, and I thank you, in Jesus' name, that you are involved. God, please orchestrate this moment and direct everyone in the room toward Ben's healing."

I reached over and grabbed the doctor's hands. "And Lord, please watch over these hands while he's working with Ben. Let the Spirit of God move in the operating room. Amen."

I hugged Ben and gave him a little kiss. Then I watched as he and the doctor went down the hall, knowing there was nothing more I could do.

■ ■ ■

The room Ben had just left was quiet and empty. This was my time to let go. I cried for a good twenty minutes. I knew I needed to be strong, but I had to shed some tears first to get there. Once again, he was going under a surgeon's knife and we had no idea what they'd find. Once again, I was hoping for a miracle.

After I'd composed myself, I called James and asked him

how to get to his church. He told me it wasn't too far from the hospital and that everyone would be waiting for me. When I arrived at the church, they were in the middle of a staff meeting. They welcomed me with embraces and a few introductions, and all of a sudden that meeting turned into a high-energy praise and worship service just for me.

There were only about a dozen people at the church, but it felt like an army. We prayed and sang for Ben's healing, thanking the Lord and asking for his protection over both Ben and me. I'd never met any of these people before, yet they showered me with love like I was one of their own.

As I looked around, I kept thinking, *God is so good. Ben has only known James for a few days. But now James's church is supporting me in a time of great need.* Nothing is a coincidence, and the Lord has never ceased to remind me of this. God orchestrated it so that I'd have support in Oakland, rather than be stuck for ten hours in that waiting room with my skin crawling from anxiety. It's like the story in Genesis 22 where God had already prepared the ram in the thicket for Abraham. God wanted me alone with Ben in the hospital, but he would comfort me with strangers at this church.

I now understood why God had said, "Go alone." He walked me through the day and took care of me, making it clear that he would never leave me or forsake me.

I thought of all this as we prayed. We continued to move in the Spirit through the room, joining our hands and feeling our souls swell in our rejoicing. But an uneasiness that I'd known all too well started to creep through my body. The scary, nervous feeling that had plagued me when I was pregnant with

Ben was back again. That feeling grew and grew, threatening to wash over my entire being. My stomach started feeling sick. I realized my fingers were beginning to tremble. Right then, I rebuked that spirit of fear in the name of Jesus.

As I kept praying, the strength I felt from the Lord started to win out. My anxiety began to subside, a little at a time, until I was finally at peace again. My stomach felt better. I breathed deeply and thanked God with every exhale.

After about three and a half hours, we concluded the praise and worship. This was one of the deepest spiritual cleansings I've felt in my life, and I thanked God once again for leading me to this church and its wonderful people. We'd had a full morning, swatting back all fears with intense prayer, and we needed some time to unwind and get to know each other better.

We headed to a beautiful restaurant near the Port of Oakland, where we all fellowshipped and laughed together. The ocean breeze felt so refreshing. My mind had been taken away from focusing on the negative and my fears about this surgery. I looked out at the water, watching the birds and the boats, thinking of my Ben. I knew he was in the hands of the Lord.

■ ■ ■

I arrived back at the hospital and found out that Ben would still be in surgery for a couple more hours. I was in waiting mode again, but at least it wouldn't be for long. I was also happy to see an unexpected show of support. While I was away at church, Denise, one of Ben's friends, had arrived at the hospital and posted herself in the waiting room with her blanket and earbuds. God bless her.

Ben actually had two procedures that day, which is why the operation took so long. The first surgery was for his brain, and the other was a sinus procedure. The surgeons started by cutting across Ben's forehead, from ear to ear, and pulling his face down. They cut a square into Ben's skull to get access to his brain. The other procedure required a surgeon to go through Ben's nose and work on his sinuses.

Ben was under the knife for more than ten hours. Toward the end of the first procedure, the brain surgeon came to the waiting room to deliver an update. I clasped my hands and prayed for good news.

"We got it all," the doctor told me with a smile. "It didn't go into the brain."

"Thank you, Jesus!" I cried out. "Oh, my God, thank you."

The doctor continued, "Ben is still in surgery with the sinus doctor."

About an hour later, that doctor came out and delivered more good news.

"We got it all," said the doctor. "Ben's in good shape."

"Hallelujah!" I shouted. "I just wish I'd had a chance to meet with you and pray with you before the surgery."

"Don't worry," the doctor said with a smile. "I pray before all of my surgeries."

I was amazed. You see, I realized right then that God knew I hadn't needed to pray with this doctor before surgery because he was already prayed up.

When I finally got to see Ben, I was taken aback by the

huge bandage around his head. His forehead was puffy from fluid buildup. One of his eye sockets was black-and-blue, like he'd been punched. Both sockets were so swollen that they'd shut completely.

Ben slowly started to wake up.

"Baby, can you hear me?" I asked him. "Are you okay?"

Ben took a deep breath.

"Mom, I'm hungry. Can you have them bring me something to eat?"

"Ben, you're so crazy, wanting to eat already! Let's wait and see what the doctors say. How does your head feel?"

"It feels like there's apple juice in my forehead."

"Apple juice?"

"Yeah, Mom, apple juice. So when can I eat?"

That "apple juice" was cerebrospinal fluid pooling in the space where a piece of Ben's skull had been removed. Obviously his brain was fine because that boy was talking as crazy as ever. I couldn't have been happier.

■ ■ ■

Ben stayed in the hospital for about a week. During that time, his tumor was sent to be studied by various doctors around the country so they could recommend the best follow-up treatment. In the meantime, Ben learned to cope without two senses. He'd long adapted to being blind, but this surgery had indeed destroyed his sense of smell. That was tricky because so much of our sense of taste is related to our ability to smell. That's why food tastes so bland when you have a stuffy nose or a head cold. But in the grand scheme of things, losing his sense of smell was a small price to pay. Ben was alive and healing fast. The "apple juice" in his head soon subsided, and his eye sockets returned to normal.

Ben looked different after his surgery. He'd always loved having braids, but the front part of his head had been shaved. Ben insisted on keeping what few braids were left on the back of his head. I told him he looked like the Predator, the freaky alien from the science fiction movies. Anndrya ended up cutting off the remaining braids, leaving Ben with a shiny bald head.

Three weeks after the surgery, everything started looking sketchy again. An MRI showed the tumor was growing back. The doctors recommended chemotherapy right away because this cancer was looking unusually aggressive.

It felt like we'd gone back to square one. The doctors wanted to use the same chemotherapy treatment Ben had received when he was two years old. I remembered his hair falling out and the endless doctor's appointments. It made me sick thinking about it.

Once again, Ben would need a catheter in his chest to get that sickening poison into his system. He just rolled with this news at first, and we all kept praying with healing Scriptures to get through this latest chapter of Ben's health. I'd say, "Ben, you're already healed, right?" And he'd say, "Yup, I know."

CHAPTER 21

MEMORIES OF PARADISE

At last, a bit of paradise. Within a few months of Ben's brain and sinus surgery—and with one chemotherapy treatment under his belt—we were off to Hawaii. Ben had been invited to speak at New Hope Christian Fellowship in Honolulu, which has five services each weekend and brings together more than fourteen thousand people at its church campuses around the Hawaiian Islands.

A boy Ben's age named Danny went to the church. He'd shared an Internet clip of Ben with his father, Mike, who was very active in the congregation. Danny said Ben was the kind of person who should come speak there. About four months later, Ben was invited to share his testimony.

We stayed in Hawaii for five days. Ben spoke at two services on Saturday and three on Sunday, wearing a Hawaiian lei around his neck and testifying about his devotion to God.

At one point, Pastor Wayne Cordeiro asked Ben, "Do you ever feel frustrated and ask God, 'Why?'"

"I've done that plenty of times," Ben said, "just saying 'why?' out of nowhere. But then again I made a promise never to ask 'why?' and never to say 'but.'"

Then Ben explained that he had never lost his faith in God. Sometimes, he admitted, "in my flesh, I feel like, 'Just forget it.' But in my spirit, it'll just be like, 'Ben, we're going to get through this. Don't even trip. Let's keep going.'"

The crowd reacted with laughter and applause to that. In fact, Ben drew the people to him with his personality and the love he showed toward everyone. In addition to the thousands of people who heard him live at each service, many more listened as the service was streamed over the Internet. As Ben was speaking during one video stream, a comment came through from a woman in Japan who wrote, "Ben, now that I see you, I know God is real."

At the end of each service, Ben signed a bunch of cards, postcards, and T-shirts that he and I had brought with us. I couldn't believe how many people were lined up to meet Ben, like he was a movie star. One of those people in line was Danny. The crowd was so overwhelming that Danny never made it to the front. He told his dad that it was okay, he didn't have to meet Ben. He was just glad Ben came to their church.

When we got back to the hotel, a woman from the church called and asked if Ben wanted to go surfing. Of course Ben said, "Oh, yeah!" That lady then called Danny to see if he'd like to take Ben surfing, and it was like they'd both won the lottery. Those two hit it off immediately. Danny's family invited Ben to stay with them for a couple of days. Once Ben told Danny that he'd brought his Wii from home, there was no stopping them.

I spent those days back at the hotel and was able to do some sightseeing of my own. During the day, I'd go shopping and exploring, and we'd all meet up for a nice dinner. I'd never been to Hawaii, and it was just the paradise I'd imagined. The weather was so nice and warm. I'd never seen ocean water looking that crystal clear. The sandy beaches went for miles, and my ears were soothed by the sounds of the crashing surf. After all the drama during the last couple of months, this was the perfect way to connect with the Lord and unwind.

On the day Ben went surfing in Waikiki, someone at the church called KGMB TV in Honolulu and invited them to film a segment on Ben. The truth is, I wasn't crazy about the idea of Ben going surfing. The doctors had given Ben strict orders not to get his catheter dirty because a blood infection could be fatal. But the pull of the surf was just too enticing for Ben, and I didn't want to deny him an opportunity that might not come our way again. To protect his chest catheter from the seawater, I bought some plastic covering to shield the opening.

As Ben prepared to get in the water, I watched him pop the cap off his catheter. The first words that came into my mind were *instant death*.

"No, Ben!" I said. "Don't you remember what the doctor said?"

"But, Mom, you're the one who told me to have faith!"

"I said have faith in God, but don't test him!"

I screwed the cap back on, and Ben took off like a shot. He was already halfway in the water, so he might as well go and have fun. Ben was all decked out in his shorts and blue tank top with a surfboard by his side. Since a camera crew was out there as well, I whispered, "Okay, Ben, don't embarrass me. You better get on that board and ride it!" He just laughed.

Ben paddled out into the water along with the instructor and other students. Though water had frightened him as a child, the smile on Ben's face now was as wide as that Pacific Ocean horizon.

A wave started to rise, just big enough that it could support a surfboard. That was Ben's cue. As the wave came through, he stood straight up on his board and found his balance. The next thing I knew, he was surfing on that beautiful blue ocean water. He rode all the way in until he nearly reached the shore. I yelled, "You go, boy!"

I'll never forget that image of Ben, upright on a surfboard with his arms outstretched, like a bird soaring to some heavenly place. After all we'd been through—the surgeries and stitches, the pain of catheter tubes and being fitted for prosthetic eyes—this was one of my proudest moments as his mother.

■ ■ ■

Ben's doctor didn't share our thrill of Ben surfing for the first time.

We returned from Hawaii on a Wednesday, and Ben went back to school the following day. After his first day back, Ben came home and said he'd been having hot and cold flashes during class. I told him to get his stuff because we were going to the hospital. Most of the time Ben would start fussing if we had to take a last-minute trip to the doctor. This time, Ben didn't fight me. He knew something was up.

Ben spent eleven days in intensive care. For the first several days, the doctors were just trying to figure out what was going on. Ben had three different types of bacteria in his blood. They were able to identify two of the bacteria, but the third was a mystery. That made it tough to know which antibiotics or other medication Ben should take. They were kind of flabbergasted.

"Where has this kid been?" one of the doctors asked.

"Surfing in Hawaii," I admitted.

The doctor shot me a look that told me he wasn't too happy about this news. But at least they knew to look for a marine bacteria. Soon after the doctors got this information, they were finally able to identify that last bacteria and treat Ben to the fullest.

This was the only life that Ben would ever live, so why not go surfing? They might have said I was putting Ben in danger, but his life was already in danger. Come on, he had cancer. Let him enjoy every day. Ben didn't have to go surfing, but he did. And it was worth it for both of us. Thank God that he had the chance.

Ben had even told the KGMB reporter, "With God on my side, pretty soon I'll be walking on that water."

■ ■ ■

Throughout his fight, Ben was encouraged by the support he received from many of his friends, as well as the wider community. On the day the final Harry Potter book was released, Mrs. Akiyama brought Ben a copy of the book in braille—it actually came in two boxes because braille books are huge. They agreed to see which one of them could finish the book first. As they were reading, they'd touch base each day to see which part each of them was on and to talk about what had happened in the story. I was glad to see his mind moving while we went through those draining hospital stays. Plus, it reminded me that Ben was still just like any other kid at some level. Everyone was reading Harry Potter, and so was he.

Ben told Mrs. Akiyama about a dream he'd had where he was carrying a bunch of heavy suitcases. None of them belonged to him, but he carried them anyway. Finally, he put them down.

"I think I'm carrying burdens for other people," said Ben. "I put the suitcases down, and so I'm putting their burdens down by putting my burdens down."

The *Sacramento Bee* wrote more stories about Ben, including a lengthy piece about the reoccurrence of his cancer. The paper had written numerous other stories, too, including brief accounts about Ben's appearance on *The Ellen DeGeneres Show* and his stint as grand marshal for our local Elk Grove Western Festival parade.

By now, Ben felt sick a lot. I started wondering why the Lord said this experience "wasn't for me." It was all for his glory, but now I asked the Lord, *Ben's going through this terrible ordeal, and you're going to take him away?* I talked to God like he was my dad. I needed to have peace with all of this.

Ben barely got sick when he went through chemotherapy as a toddler, but this time was different. The longer the treatments went on, the sicker he got. It was a gradual thing. He reminded me of a big balloon that was slowly leaking air. He'd have to spend four days of each month in the hospital, hooked up to bags of chemicals. The first day would usually be fine, but after that the side effects would take hold.

But we had more traveling to do. Ben was invited to speak at the People, Ideas, Nature, Creativity (PINC) Conference in Amsterdam in May 2008. The conference draws about five hundred people from all over the world. Its purpose is to inspire creative thinking for all kinds of professionals, including those in business and science. We were only in Amsterdam for about four days, but we had so much fun. I knew nothing about this city, but the people were friendly and seemed especially in awe of Ben. Despite being in the midst of chemotherapy treatments, Ben was on his A-game.

We also got some time to sightsee, and the experience was captured by a news camera crew. As we walked through the shopping district, Ben was surprised at how narrow the cobblestone streets were. He said something like, "That's a street? That's a hop and a step. It's not even a skip!" The crew filmed Ben clicking his way through the area, and he pointed out every time they passed a pillar. Ben's clicking sounded really strong and rhythmic—*click CLICK, click CLICK, click CLICK*—like he was throwing one-two punches with his tongue.

Ben took his sound awareness a step further. He noticed that one of the pillars was round, and he could even tell if a building he passed was made of brick, just from the sound of the echo. Ben also showed off his ability to use a revolving door.

■ ■ ■

That summer Ben and I returned to Camp Okizu, where he could connect with some other kids fighting cancer. When we'd gone the year before, Ben had lost his iPod. So this year I told him, "You're going to leave your iPod in the car." He fought me on that, but I explained that I wasn't about to buy that boy yet another iPod.

Our cabin was on the lowest part of the hill, and it was way too dark to see the trail that ran from the main lodge to our cabin. I wasn't looking forward to finding my way. "Ben, I don't know how to get to our cabin," I said. "It's dark, and I'm scared. Can you take me?"

Ben chuckled.

"I will if you let me get my iPod out of the car."

"No, Ben!" I said. "I already told you the iPod is going to stay there."

"C'mon, Mom. Just let me get the iPod, and I'll take you. I promise I won't lose it."

"Forget it!" I said, before stomping off. "I'll go by myself!"

Slowly, I made my way down the hill. I couldn't see anything, and all the rustling branches and forest sounds were starting to unnerve me. Was a bear going to jump out from behind a tree? As I kept walking through the darkness, my eyes played tricks on me. It looked like something was popping on the ground in front of me. I felt my feet begin to slip as the hill got steeper.

I got so scared that I turned around and ran back up the hill. At that high elevation, I was having a hard time breathing. I kept thinking, *Oh no, they're going to find me dead in the morning!*

I eventually made it back to the lodge. I was so mad at Ben that I couldn't even speak. I also couldn't speak because I was still trying to catch my breath. I found a couch and flopped on top of it. Ben was in the other room playing games with some kids and having all the fun in the world. Everybody was hyped up because it was the first night of camp. I figured I'd wait for Ben, but judging by all the laughing, I could tell he wasn't going anywhere for a long time.

Finally I heard one of the other parents say she was going to find our cabin, and so I decided to tag along. I walked back down the hill thinking how funny it was that I had first asked a kid who couldn't see to lead me to our cabin.

CHAPTER 22

MIRACULOUS GIFTS

BEN SPENT New Year's Eve 2007 in the hospital. He said it was all right if I wanted to go out and celebrate, because he was going to have fun with the other kids. Ben and a friend in the hospital named Austin staged wheelchair races around the pediatric ward.

A nurse took me aside one day and said, "Your son, Ben— he's an angel." She was impressed by how easygoing and undemanding he was.

I'd left my evening job at the DMV so I could spend nights at the hospital with Ben. His treatment called for four days of chemotherapy followed by a break for a few weeks. This continued for months, and the longer the treatment went on, the sicker Ben became. His appetite started to wither away, and it didn't help that his sense of smell was gone. This boy could usually eat like a racehorse, but after a while he didn't even crave his favorite treats. I brought Ben some beef sticks and a bag of Skittles candy, but they ended up sitting there for a week before I finally threw them away. Many people going through chemotherapy have their sense of taste altered, and this was especially true of Ben. Whenever he was ready to eat, Ben would take a bite and say it tasted nasty.

This was no way for him to live.

"I'm so tired of being sick," Ben said to me. "I'd rather die."

Ben was getting noticeably weaker. The chemotherapy treatments were leaving him a lot more tired than usual, and I wasn't sure how much more he'd be able to handle. I still wanted to have an extra-special birthday celebration though. Oh, it turned out to be special all right.

Ben invited Stevie Wonder to a sixteenth birthday party at our house on January 26, 2008. Stevie said he'd be there. It was that simple. I thought it was so sweet of him to take the time to visit Ben. He knew what Ben was going through and came to show his support like a true friend.

Knowing that Stevie was coming over, I cooked some soul food for him, including my sweet potato pie. A bunch of Ben's friends had gathered in the house, which we'd decorated with balloons. We even got a DJ and a dance floor ready to go. Stevie pulled up in a car with one of his assistants, and the kids flocked around him when he came into the house. As a gift, Stevie brought Ben a high-tech electronic scanner that reads book pages aloud. We'd looked at this device together the day we met Stevie at the technology expo. It cost over $7,000. That's the kind of giving person Stevie is.

We sat around the table and ate. Stevie couldn't stop

raving about my sweet potato pie. And he was so great with Ben's friends. Stevie took pictures with all the kids. The DJ had a microphone, so Stevie sang "Happy Birthday," a track from his 1980 album *Hotter than July* about Martin Luther King Jr.

The fact that this song was a little before Ben's time led to a funny moment at the party. During one of the verses, Stevie handed the microphone over and said, "Here, Ben, sing!" Ben laughed and yelled, "I don't know that song!" Stevie laughed, too, and replied, "Well then, gimme back the microphone!"

I thought it was hilarious that Ben straight up told Stevie that he didn't know his song. Who does that? No matter what, those two were so comfortable with each other. They were so much alike, and not just because they were both blind. They were thoughtful, funny, and spiritual people with a lot of love to give.

Stevie's also very independent like Ben. He was going upstairs to check out Ben's room or something, and immediately I said, "You don't need help?" He said, "No, I got it. I'm good."

I don't think Stevie wants to be coddled, even though he has people on standby to help him. At one point when we were eating, Stevie dropped something and his assistant picked it up quick, not even giving Stevie a chance to do it. If Stevie were just with me, I'd be thinking, *You better pick that up.* Oh, all Stevie needs is a month with me, and he'd be doing it all himself!

Ben's energy was very up-and-down at the party. He'd

dance for a little bit before having to go lie back down. I'd nudge Ben, saying, "Get up! Stevie came all this way to see you!" Stevie assured me that it was okay and to let Ben be. He understood that Ben wasn't feeling 100 percent and was just happy to be there for his young friend.

That night Stevie and I talked for a long time. We talked about all kinds of things—faith, family, and my recipe for sweet potato pie. He told me that I reminded him of his mother. I took that as a real compliment.

One thing about Stevie—and probably a lot of other musicians too—is that he's a night owl. By 3 a.m. the party was over, and Ben was asleep. But Stevie and I were still talking. I wanted to keep sitting up with him, but my eyes just couldn't stay open any longer. I offered him a bed in our house, but he had a hotel nearby. The next day Stevie came back to spend a little more time with us before heading back to Los Angeles.

We couldn't have wished for a better sixteenth birthday for Ben.

■ ■ ■

The chemotherapy was continuous and draining, yet Ben always tried to make the best of it. He'd bring his own chili, cheese, and hot dogs to the hospital, along with a can opener. Ben also brought one of his video game systems and would challenge other kids on his floor. He'd have a lot of fun joking with the nurses, trying to sucker them into massaging his size 13 feet. Ben's room was always alive, and people would brighten up when he came around.

Ben liked to watch movies or Japanese cartoons at night in the hospital when everyone else on the floor was asleep. I slept in his room on a sofa bed.

One night, I came into his room at about midnight. Ben asked me to stay up and watch the *Avatar* cartoon with him. I told him it was getting late and we could watch it in the morning. It was time to get some rest.

Ben startled me awake at about five the next morning.

"Mom! Wake up!"

At first I thought I was just dreaming.

"Mom! Wake up! Something happened to me!"

I rolled over. Ben was more amped up than I'd seen him in weeks.

"Ben, I'm awake. What is it?"

"The nurse was in here massaging my feet, and she stopped to get more lotion. When she let go, time stood still."

Now he had my attention. I knew we were in the presence of something holy. Ben continued: "When the nurse turned around to get the lotion, two people grabbed my feet. Oh, Mom, it felt so good! They massaged my feet for such a long time too. When the nurse turned back around, they both let go."

"Ben, those were angels," I said.

"I know."

"Did you see them?"

"No, Mom. I had my eyes closed."

Ben and I didn't talk a lot more about it, but I was so grateful for this reminder from the Lord that he was with Ben and was taking care of my son.

■ ■ ■

We hoped that radiation would help kill Ben's tumor for good, but this process was extremely uncomfortable. For his first round of treatments, Ben was fitted with a mesh mask that made him very claustrophobic. It almost looked like he was wearing chain-mail armor over his face. Ben said it felt like he was being held against his will.

The doctors also used gamma-knife radiosurgery, a process in which about two hundred beams of radiation are focused precisely on a tumor or other target. The upside is that this sophisticated technique allows doctors to perform procedures on the brain without having to cut anything open. The downside for Ben was that this approach was even more uncomfortable than the mesh mask. First, a lightweight frame was placed over his head. It was made of a horizontal metal bar and two vertical metal bars that screwed into his forehead. As the radiation was administered, the frame kept his head stabilized.

For all its discomfort, this procedure worked well at first. The doctors would get right on top of Ben's sinus tumor with the gamma-knife radiation, and that would make the tumor go away. That's when I'd start rejoicing and think, *Thank you, Jesus!*

But the next round of tests would show that the tumor had come back. I was terrified about a tumor forming on Ben's brain. I also worried about the possible side effects of treatment. Every time the doctors blasted a tumor with radiation, the MRI chart showed a black hole in the spot where he was being treated. I didn't want Ben's brain to be eaten up like that. He was an incredibly smart kid who had lots of deep thoughts, and I would be devastated to see him lose who he was.

When the chemotherapy and radiation didn't seem to be working, we tried experimental dietary supplements called glyconutrients. These sugar pills are purported to have healing powers for those fighting cancer and other diseases. Their effectiveness has yet to be proven, but when you're the parent of a child fighting cancer, you'll try almost anything if you think it might help. I'd read about these supplements online, and anything that gave us a chance to fight Ben's cancer without that poisonous chemotherapy sounded good to me.

Those pills were incredibly expensive, about $600 a month, and my insurance didn't cover the cost. We held fund-raisers so Ben could afford to keep taking them. One of my coworkers helped organize a car wash. A neighbor held a party fund-raiser at his house and raised about $1,500. One lady there wrote a check for $500 and handed it to Ben. We were touched by everyone's kindness and support, but the pills didn't work.

I still believed Ben would be healed. As a mother, you can't give up hope. But you do have to come to a realization that it is what it is. You will kill yourself if you continue to fight for something you can't control. In the end, we're all on God's time.

All of these treatments were trial and error, and I felt helpless in not being able to do more. I was waiting for the Lord to speak to me again, like the time he told me that Ben "would live and not die." It wasn't happening this time around. None of this was anything I could fix. I knew I just had to get through it, but how?

I'd sometimes call Sister Devon in Alabama and tell her how tired I was from this fight. Ben was becoming more adamant that he didn't want to continue the chemotherapy and radiation treatments. Sister Devon and I were both going through a heavy time. She had lost her oldest son in an accident, so she could understand what I was going through. I was so heartbroken for my Sister Devon when her son passed and did my best to support her however I could. We may never know why some people come into our lives, but there's always a reason. Sister Devon told me she thanked God that he put us together, and I couldn't agree more.

She counseled me to think about what Ben wanted and to consider how tired he might be—and how selfish we sometimes are. We all wanted Ben here, but maybe he wanted to go home and be with the Lord. I hadn't really thought of it like that. Instead of trying to put up a fight, she encouraged me to think about how I could make him comfortable, to think about his needs instead of my wants.

■ ■ ■

Despite all the hardships and his draining health, Ben tried to act like none of this was really happening. He'd go straight from radiation treatments to school. He'd do his best to hang in there for the whole day. Sometimes he could, and sometimes he couldn't.

Ben would walk home with a friend, who would always

offer to carry Ben on his back, or at least to carry his backpack for him. Ben always said, "No, I got it," and kept on moving.

The school nurse reserved a bed in her office for Ben to use when he was too weak or ill to keep going to classes. On those days, his math teacher, Ms. Stuart, or the campus police officer would give him a ride home.

My hurts and weaknesses were getting the better of me. Maybe I just needed to hear Ben say, "Mom, I'm dying." But he had it handled. As he told Pastor Cordeira when we were in Hawaii, "When I was going through the surgery and stuff, God just told me, 'Kick back and relax,' and that's all I've been doing ever since." Ben was never overwhelmed by fear or sorrow.

So it was up to me to handle my sadness. Even though I knew other parents with kids who had cancer, I didn't feel like I could relate to them. Everyone's case is different, and there weren't any words anyone could say to make me feel better.

One morning, feeling the weight of Ben's health on my mind, I called in to a show on Christian radio. For thirty-five dollars, you could talk to a counselor over the phone, and I figured they knew what they were doing and could help me. I didn't know how to release this frustrating feeling that I was lost as to how to deal with Ben's worsening condition.

My son has cancer, and the treatments are making him
*   wither away.*
The doctors are trying their best, but nothing
*   is curing Ben.*

*The Bible tells me to cast my burdens and cares upon God,
and he'll take care of them.*
But how exactly do I give this over to God?
*What will it truly take so I won't have to deal with this
anymore?*
If Ben dies, will I ever be able to find peace?

All of these thoughts flooded my mind while I stayed on hold. I waited . . . and waited . . . for over an hour, until my phone started dying. Finally, I hung up.

As I put the phone down, the Lord reminded me, *I am your counselor. I am all you need.*

Though nobody else was home, I went into my room, closed the door, and let everything I'd been bottling up come rushing out. My hands were soaked from sobbing into them, and my bloodshot eyes stung with salty tears. I'd cried so hard that I was left exhausted, collapsed on my bed and struggling to catch my breath.

I poured out my heart to God. "This hurts so much, and it's so heavy. Lord, I need you right now." I trusted him, but I had been expecting to hear God like I did years before when Ben lost both his eyes to cancer.

"God! You said to cast my cares upon you—but how, Lord, am I supposed to do that? My baby is dying! I'll tell you what. *You* get into the car and drive him to the doctor. I'm not doing it anymore! *You* do it!"

In that moment, God brought to mind the prayer that Jesus taught his disciples: "Our Father which art in heaven, hallowed be thy name. . . ."

I felt as if the next lines had been written just for me: "Thy kingdom come, thy will be done in earth, as it is in heaven. . . ." And as I prayed that the Lord's will, rather than mine, be done when it came to Ben's future, an overwhelming peace came upon me. My breathing started to relax, and tears stopped falling from my eyes. I had this unshakable assurance that God would never leave or forsake me. I had given myself over to God and left all my trust with him. I expelled the hurt from me so he could handle it. God let me know that he was in control.

My prayer changed from that moment.

I wasn't asking for the Lord to heal Ben anymore. Now my prayer was, *Lord, let your will be done. And whatever your will is, even if Ben goes home with you today, please give me the perfect peace that surpasses all understanding. I need to be at peace, whether it's in Ben's life or death. It doesn't matter which way it goes.*

Waves of calmness flowed throughout my body. I knew God had heard me—and would carry me all the way.

CHAPTER 23

DROPPING ALL THE BURDENS

ALL THE NASTY CHEMICALS from the chemotherapy were sucking the life out of Ben. He spent a lot of time talking with Sister Devon, telling her how tired he felt and how much he hated the treatments. He also didn't want me to be sad. Sister Devon encouraged Ben to talk with me more about his wishes, but he kept a lot of his feelings to himself. Although I know Ben loved me, I think he felt that this situation was something to reconcile privately between himself and God.

Ben brought video games with him to the chemotherapy treatments, but he got so weak that he didn't play them much. Then he started aching all over. It was so horrible that Ben became even more convinced that he didn't want any more treatments. It wasn't like Ben to give up, so I knew he was feeling more pain than we could imagine.

We didn't have many options left. Sister Devon counseled me again to think of Ben's wishes and consider his comfort before all else. She said that maybe Ben was ready to go home to the Lord. He might be young in years, she told me, but I should consider the full life he'd led, all the places he'd been, and all the people he'd touched. He had experienced more than many people three times his age had. Sister Devon reminded me that elderly people aren't the only ones who've lived a full life. Think of Jesus, she said—he was only thirty-three when he died.

"I don't want to be sick," Ben would tell me. "I'm done taking the treatments. This isn't how I'm supposed to live."

"But if you stop them, you know what that means?" I'd remind him.

"Yes, Mom. I know."

"Well, we're just going to have to enjoy every day we've got left."

Later in the year, after talking more with Ben and then thinking and praying hard about his situation, I told the doctor that Ben was done with chemotherapy, that it seemed to be doing him more harm than good. The doctor gave us a sad and hurt look, like we were quitting the fight of our lives. I just felt that Ben deserved better than this. The doctor respected our wishes, but I could tell he was unhappy with Ben's decision. I said that if these were Ben's last days, we were just going to enjoy life. That would be our objective with whatever time was left.

The doctor didn't give up. He called me when we got home and said there was one more chemotherapy option we should definitely consider. It wasn't normally used with the kind of tumor Ben had; however, it didn't make people as sick. Ben agreed to try it. Sure enough, with this treatment Ben didn't get sick and he was able to eat a little. My hopes started rising again, but there was only so much I could do to convince myself that Ben would return to his usual self.

■ ■ ■

Ben's health took a dark turn around Thanksgiving of 2008. We'd spent that holiday weekend in Las Vegas for a family gathering. Going to the Strip wasn't our idea of a good time, but we took Ben down there briefly. He was in a wheelchair because he'd had a hard time walking. I figured this latest chemotherapy had made him weak. I didn't realize how much he was struggling. Ben wasn't going to tell me if he was, anyway. Maybe I didn't want to admit that he was dying.

Ben had a doctor's appointment a few weeks after we returned home. By then, he had dropped a lot of weight. My muscular, five-foot-eight-inch son had withered to skin and bones. I told the doctor that Ben had been having trouble walking for the past month and was hardly eating. The doctor ordered an MRI as I braced myself for the worst. And that's basically the news we got.

The tumor had disappeared from Ben's sinuses, but the cancer had mutated and settled into his spinal fluid. That's why Ben was having so much trouble walking.

The doctor gave us a sorrowful look that said, *There's nothing else we can do.* He told us we might as well stop chemotherapy because Ben's body wasn't responding to treatments anymore.

I clenched my hands and thought, *This is it. Your baby's getting ready to die, and you have to prepare yourself for this.* I needed to know how much time might be left, how much more Ben might have to suffer before he was finally at peace.

"So, doctor, what's going to happen now?" I asked.

"With this kind of cancer Ben will probably start sleeping a lot," he said. "And then he'll just sleep more and more until he doesn't wake up."

"Ben, how do you feel about this?" I said.

"Oh, so I'm just going to go to sleep?" Ben responded calmly. "That's cool with me."

Ben was ready to die. He'd long resolved himself to the idea, and I couldn't understand it. I don't think anybody could. Ben never questioned God's purpose, even when God called people home. Ben knew that being called to heaven was a greater gift than anything that could be found on earth. I needed to start thinking that way too.

■ ■ ■

I walked to the parking lot in a fog. *Oh my goodness. This is it. I'm really going to lose him.* So many emotions flooded my mind as I tried to wrap my head around the idea that Ben was going to die. It was just a matter of time now.

I went to fetch our truck and pick up Ben in front of the hospital. My hands trembled as I fumbled with the keys, trying to open the door. Sitting in the driver's seat, I closed the door and took in the silence. My fear and sadness had been welling up and were about to explode like a ton of dynamite. Slowly, tears started streaming down my face, until I held my head in my hands and started screaming.

"Lord! Lord! Lord!" I wailed over and over.

My life and hope came crashing down. All of those moments I'd tried to be strong . . . all of those times I'd kept my sadness inside so Ben wouldn't worry. . . . A mother could only take so much.

I did my best to catch my breath and compose myself. I didn't want Ben to know I'd been crying, though my puffy, red eyes would give me away to anyone else. I pulled up to the front of the hospital, where Ben was waiting in a wheelchair with his brother Isaiah. Both of them were acting like this was just some routine visit to the doctor.

Ben sat in the passenger seat, singing a little gospel and just relaxing on the ride. My emotions started bubbling up again. This time I was getting mad. I wanted to shake Ben and say, "Boy, what is wrong with you?" The more nonchalant Ben acted, the more frustrated I felt. What was going through his mind? Was he scared? I had to do *something*. What could I do?

Ben continued singing to himself as we drove home in the darkness. I finally had to find out from him what was going on in his heart and mind. I turned off the music.

"Ben, all jokes aside, aren't you afraid to die?"

"No, Mom," he said.

"Seriously—you don't need me to hold you and cry with you?"

"No."

My throat started to pinch, and tears filled my eyes. I couldn't hold it in any longer.

"Well, I need to cry in front of you," I said.

"Go ahead, Mom."

That's all the permission I needed. I sobbed and sobbed some more, even as I kept driving home. I'd been holding this inside for so long. But no matter how much I cried, Ben sat there silently, waiting for me to get all the tears out.

"Mom, why are you crying?" he finally asked. "What's the deal?"

"Ben, I won't be able to touch you!" I said through my tears. "I won't be able to be near you. I won't be able to braid your hair. I won't be able to smell you. I won't be able to hear you!"

He said nothing.

"You know, Ben, I never wanted to cry in front of you."

"It's okay. I always knew when you cried anyway."

■ ■ ■

Ben was so weak when we got home that he had to be carried upstairs. He was as helpless as if he were a baby again.

It's easy to get selfish and say, "I don't want you to die," but you can't stop a person from dying. You can only help comfort him. Ben had told me that he couldn't do it anymore, that he was just too sick. "It's okay, baby," I assured him. But we didn't give up. Rather, we gave it to God.

Since Ben had survived cancer before, Isaiah thought his brother was going to make it. As Ben's health continued to slip, Isaiah felt increasingly frustrated. He started getting angry easily and kept saying he didn't want to be bothered. He had a hard time concentrating at school. It was a lot for a thirteen-year-old boy to see his big brother suffering like this.

Isaiah and Ben were as close as brothers could be. They'd shared a room for most of their lives. Even though they had bunk beds, Ben would still sometimes sleep next to Isaiah on the bottom bed. Isaiah had been Ben's guide around school, and they liked to grab burritos and soda at Taco Bell on the way home.

Over the remaining weeks, it got to the point where Ben didn't have the strength to get out of bed. He spent most of his time sleeping under his favorite blue blanket. A hospice nurse came to help take care of Ben, and we moved his bed into the family room. When Ben needed to be bathed, we'd carry him to the upstairs tub.

I'd taken a leave from work. I spent lots of time kneeling next to Ben and savoring my last moments with him. I would treasure every one of them.

Even as Ben became weaker, his friends still wanted to visit. We welcomed them all. Ben would joke, "You know I can't stop people from coming! Let them come!" Visitors were surprised that the mood in the house was never somber. We weren't sitting around with glum looks on our faces and drowning in our tears. We laughed, and we prayed. We shared food, and even though this might sound unbelievable, we had fun.

I had so many loving people helping me out and coming to support Ben. But I don't know how anyone could go through this without Christ Jesus. The peace that God gave

CHAPTER 24

SAYING GOOD-BYE

I STILL LOOK BACK on Ben's final days as a special time. I got to lie in bed with him and sleep next to him. I carried him to the upstairs tub even though he was heavy for me to lift, despite the weight he'd lost. People asked me why I didn't let the hospice nurse do it, but that was crazy. Is that what they'd do if their child was dying and these were the last times they'd be with him? I needed to be as close to Ben as possible, as often as possible.

José Luis Villegas, a photographer with the *Sacramento Bee*, came to our home to document these days for the newspaper. The one time I fell when carrying Ben happened while he was there. I was bringing him down the stairs and missed a step, and I immediately cradled Ben's head so he wouldn't get hurt.

"Oh, Ben, are you all right?"

"Yeah, Mom."

"Baby, are you sure?"

"Yes, Mom. Now will you get off me?"

Ben wasn't able to stand to urinate, so I'd help him get in a warm tub where he could push it out. He needed help to pass his bowel movements too. And after all that, I'd have to clean up Ben and put him back to bed. As much as people wanted to help, this was my son, and I would never let anyone else do this.

It was hard to see Ben reduced to skin and bones, with a low-maintenance Afro instead of the braids he'd been so proud of. He started to develop bedsores, which made me feel like I wasn't taking care of Ben well enough. The hospice nurses explained that the bedsores couldn't be helped. It's part of the process when the body starts shutting down.

A lot of people wanted to come by our house, knowing it might be their last chance to see Ben. Mrs. Barbara hadn't seen Ben much since she retired, but she stopped by a couple of times. She'd bought him more of the Harry Potter books in braille, including the volume where the great wizard Dumbledore dies. They talked about Dumbledore's death, and she sensed that Ben knew what was coming next.

One of Ben's favorite high school teachers, Ms. Stuart, even asked me if she and her husband, who was the football coach, could take Ben to their home and care for him for a week so that I could have a break. Their kindness touched me so much. Though I didn't feel like I could take them up on their offer, I suggested that they spend a night with Ben at our house sometime. And that's just what they did, taking over all his care one night so that I could get more than a couple of hours of uninterrupted sleep. A young woman named Kendra, who'd become close to Ben after meeting him at church, spent hours at our house, which enabled me to go out to shop for groceries and run other errands when I needed to.

■ ■ ■

When the Pughs came to see us, Sister Devon was very surprised to see Ben so sleepy rather than running around and being silly like his usual self. Yet even in this delicate state, Ben couldn't help ministering to other people. Sister Devon told Ben about some problems she was having with a family member, and like always, Ben listened patiently and comforted her. It was almost like Ben was her pastor. He told her, "Memaw, it's going to be okay. Just keep loving her because she is family and you know situations will always come up. Be there for her. It's the way the Lord wants it to be."

They talked on the phone a couple of weeks later, and before Ben hung up, he said to Sister Devon, "I love you so much, Memaw." It was the last time he'd speak to her.

Ben also wanted his siblings around. He told his oldest brother, Joe, that he wasn't afraid to die. In fact, he was happy to die. Ben knew exactly where he was going, so there was nothing to be afraid of. He told Joe to get right with God so he could meet him there.

It was almost exciting for Ben to die, as crazy as that sounds. It was something he wanted to do. He was one of the happiest people I ever met, so when he knew it was time to go, he was happy even about that.

The idea that Ben would die was tough for Ben's young

friends to comprehend, especially Anndrya. Those two weren't boyfriend and girlfriend anymore—they'd realized they were better off as best friends—but they were still extremely close. Ben had told her at the mall a few weeks before that he was really sick. Normally Ben never complained, so the fact that he acknowledged he wasn't feeling well made Anndrya realize how serious the situation was. As Ben got weaker and sicker, she had a hard time bringing herself to visit him. She didn't want to see him in such a fragile state. Plus, Anndrya knew that Ben would get mad if she started to get sad in front of him.

I felt bad for Anndrya. She was so hurt about Ben's situation, even with everyone trying to cheer her up. People would tell her that she'd be okay in time, but she'd say, "It's not okay. Ben's not supposed to die. I'm never going to get over this." She didn't feel like anybody understood. She'd confided so much in Ben since they'd met and would say he was her best friend forever.

Anndrya came over to see Ben after many of his chemotherapy and radiation treatments. Often he'd tell her, "You know I'm going to die."

"Ben, you're not going to die. Don't tell me that."

"Yes, I am. Maybe not now. Maybe not until next month. But it's going to happen at some point. Whenever that day comes, I'm ready. I'm not scared."

"Ben, seriously—"

"It's true. We're all going to die someday. When I die, don't cry. Whatever you do, don't cry. Be happy."

"That's easy for you to say! I'm going to be sad, you know."

"Don't be sad. You know I won't be sick anymore. I'll still be able to see you. The minute I die, I'm going straight to you."

"Well, if you die, will you promise to watch over me all the time?"

"I promise."

■ ■ ■

One night, Ben was on the couch playing a video game when Pastor Esley Simmons and his wife, Dr. Deborah Simmons, came over to visit.

"Ben, they're here to talk about your funeral," I said. "Do you want to hear about this? We can go in another room if you want."

"No, I want to hear about it," Ben said. "Just don't let them cremate me."

"Boy, you know we're not going to cremate you!"

Instead of discussing funeral plans, Ben started talking to the pastors about the play *Madea Goes to Jail*, one of his favorite Tyler Perry plays that was out on DVD. For the next half hour, everyone joked and laughed—but we had to get to business at some point.

"That's enough for now," I said. "It's getting late, and we need to talk about the funeral."

"All right then," Ben said. "You keep talking and handle your business. I'll keep playing my game."

We got back to funeral planning. One pastor had several plots at the cemetery for his family, and he offered me a plot for Ben. A couple of days later, the pastor went to a mortuary and mentioned Ben's story to one of the owners. The owner went online to read about Ben, and after seeing his story, he decided to cover the complete cost of the funeral, plot and all.

Within days, Ben was so weak he could barely talk. I could see that his last moments were coming.

■ ■ ■

We said good-bye to Ben on a cold January night.

I was in the kitchen when Ben said that he wanted to see me. I don't know if he was in any pain because he never acted like he was. While in hospice care, he never wanted to take any morphine or other drugs. He wanted to be in his right frame of mind when he died, so he could see God's glory as clearly as possible.

I knelt next to Ben and could hear his breathing becoming extremely shallow, as if his lungs were leaking air. His eyelids were puffy, and his body was a frail shell of what it once was.

"Ben, your momma is right here," I said to him gently. "I love you, Ben. I'm going to miss you so much. But I'm going to keep you right here in my heart. You will be a part of me forever, baby. And remember, when you get to heaven, don't forget to tell Jesus to save that spot next to you for your mom."

Ben reached up, tapping into what strength he had left, and placed a hand on me. He gently rubbed his hand up and down my back and arms, not saying a word. He was telling me good-bye. Though Ben couldn't move his lips, the love in his warm touch was louder than a thousand singing voices. I thanked God for that opportunity to say good-bye and to love him and hold him one last time.

Ben's brother Joe stayed up with him that night. He watched closely as Ben struggled with sickly, stuttering breaths. Ben didn't want to use the oxygen mask that was there for him if he needed it.

At around 3 a.m., Ben reached for Joe and grabbed his hand. He took a final breath, then exhaled like he was falling into a deep sleep. Joe tried to wake his brother up, but Ben went limp and stopped breathing. Joe started to panic and tried throwing water on Ben to wake him up. It was too late. Ben was already on his way to heaven.

I was startled awake by a bunch of yelling from downstairs.

"Mom! Mom! Moooooooom!"

Joe was screaming through the house. I hadn't been sleeping well, knowing this time was about to come. But when it did, the idea that Ben had taken his last breath was a peaceful one for me. It was so hard to see a person endure that much pain, so there was comfort in knowing that the Lord had finally called Ben home.

Joe was still frantic.

"Joe, calm down!" I said. "We knew this was going to happen." I gave him a hug to try and comfort him. "It's okay, son."

We gathered around Ben to give him our love. His brother Isaiah even took pictures and posed with Ben in his final resting state. Isaiah had a big smile on his face, like he was at a party. I know it sounds a little strange, but this is the way Ben taught us to live.

I called the pastor to say that Ben had passed away. He came over quickly, and we ended up having a service right there over Ben's body, praising the Lord and singing one of

Ben's favorite songs, "Here I Am to Worship." The opening words held special meaning for us now: "Light of the world, you stepped down into darkness, opened my eyes, let me see . . ."

We sang and prayed until the sun came up, loving one another and celebrating like Ben would have wanted. The hard part was calling the hospice and telling them that Ben had passed and that his body was ready to be taken away. They showed up not too long after, covered Ben with a sheet, and rolled him out. His brothers cried.

Yet the way Ben died gave everyone peace. The joy I felt at knowing he had awakened in Jesus' presence with his sight restored is something I can't put into words. Ben had prepared everybody and was never afraid. We weren't going to be sad, because Ben wasn't sad. Everyone felt his energy and let that sustain us when he passed. I never knew that watching death could have left me joyful.

CHAPTER 25

A NEW LIFE

HARVEST CHURCH, ELK GROVE, CALIFORNIA:
JANUARY 26, 2009

Ben's life had come full circle. We buried my son on what would have been his seventeenth birthday.

Attending the funeral of your own young child is probably the hardest thing a parent can go through. But I wasn't going to wallow in tragedy on this day. Ben's memorial service would be uplifting and focused on love, for Ben taught us all how to face death with dignity and joy. He was an example of how our time on earth pales in comparison to the everlasting life that awaits the saved in God's Kingdom.

So we weren't having a service where everyone would be moaning and dressed in black. We were going to celebrate my boy's life the way Ben would've wanted: with laughter, with music, with love and fellowship, with praise to the Lord.

I was overwhelmed by the turnout for Ben's service. More

than two thousand people came to Harvest Church in Elk Grove to support Joe, Tiffany, Derius, Isaiah, and me as we said good-bye to Ben. Many were longtime friends, such as Mrs. Barbara and Mrs. Akiyama, along with our extended family. Lots of Ben's classmates from Sheldon High School came as well. Some had never met Ben personally but were so inspired by what they saw on TV that they felt compelled to be there. It was standing room only, with people spilling into the aisles.

I had Ben dressed in a tie and light-green shirt. His brother Joe wore the same outfit and also had the letters "B-E-N" colored into the back of his head. Ben's hair had grown into a puffy Afro over the previous months, but one of my friends braided it for the service. Ben loved his braids, so this was the perfect way to send him off.

Isaiah and I both wore white as a sign of Ben's everlasting light and hope, with red flowers on our lapels. Balloons were arched over Ben's casket and the pulpit. One by one, Ben's loved ones walked to the casket and said good-bye.

Pastor Pugh and Sister Devon had traveled from Alabama to be at the service. "He looks so peaceful," I told Sister Devon. "It was hard at first, but I'm glad I didn't try to force him to do anything he didn't want to do. I know that Ben is with God. He lived a full life."

Many of Ben's young friends had a hard time seeing him in an open casket. I could understand that. They were all so young, and your friends aren't supposed to die when you're barely old enough to drive. That's when everyone's making plans for the future, falling in love, getting ready to enter college or the workforce. The mom in me didn't want to see

Ben lying in a casket either. But my will wasn't God's will, and I had learned to accept that.

Isaiah was having an especially hard time keeping it together. He felt lost without Ben. Isaiah had tried to be strong for Ben, and he felt unsure whether or not he should cry at the funeral. He couldn't help it. Isaiah cried a lot for his brother.

My love in the Lord is what preserved my strength and provided my comfort in this time that every parent would dread. I knew I could get through this day, and all the days beyond, with his support.

■ ■ ■

Stevie Wonder was among those celebrating Ben's life, and his presence brought some extra excitement to the service. Stevie had traveled to Sacramento after performing the previous week at President Barack Obama's inauguration in Washington, DC. I was touched that he'd made that effort to be a part of this special day.

I took a seat in the front row. My son Joe sat on my right, and Stevie sat next to me on the left. A church band was all ready to go. I couldn't help but feel excited to celebrate Ben's life.

"God is a good God," said Pastor Perry Kallevig in his welcoming remarks. "One of the reasons I know that's true is because God gave us someone as wonderful as Ben Underwood."

Amen to that.

Pastor Kallevig had been at our house the day before Ben died. He said he'd been having a tough time earlier that day and felt kind of blue—until he came to visit Ben. He recalled sitting at the edge of Ben's bed, knowing that my son's time was short. Ben could hardly move, so the pastor shifted him to a more comfortable position. Ben asked to have his arms scratched, which the pastor did for the next forty-five minutes or so. Ben was getting all silly and saying, "Oh, that feels good. . . . No, scratch over there. Oh yeah, stay there. Wait, now go down a little."

The crowd roared as Pastor Kallevig told this story.

Pastor Kallevig reflected on how being with Ben, even in his weakest state, helped melt away all the pastor's burdens and cares. He'd felt the essence of Ben's fun-loving spirit, which shone even in his last hours.

"Whatever load I was carrying that day, that load was being lifted in that moment," said Pastor Kallevig. "You can spend hours talking to a therapist, but usually the Lord can solve your problems in a moment if you give them to him. God ministered to me through Ben that day."

What more would have been in store if Ben had had more time? Looking around the packed church, it was clear that in his short life, Ben had become an ambassador for the blind who brought so much hope and help to people.

■ ■ ■

Later in the service, Sister Devon Pugh spoke of being in the hospital with me when Ben was born, and again before he lost his second eye to surgery. She recalled bringing him crayons and paper so she could review colors with him. As she did, she prayed that he might remember his colors after going blind. Sister Devon said that she had asked Ben a couple of years before he died if he remembered those colors, but Ben said no.

Sister Devon explained how after this conversation, the Lord put a wonderful poem in her heart, which she wrote the day after Ben passed. She read it as a gracious tribute to Ben. The poem, "He Colored My World," began,

> *Wishing you could see what I saw.*
> *The colors that God created in my world*
> *Only few have seen,*
> *Every one marked in brilliancy of awe.*
> *Colors inspired me to live, and to love,*
> *Compelling me to reverence him above. . . .*

I was touched to see how much creativity Ben sparked in other people. One of Ben's friends, Brionna Lewis, read a two-part poem called "Hope" that was inspired by him. She wrote the first part in 2007, when Ben got sick from his cancer treatments, as a way to express her support. The second half was written after Ben passed away, and it spoke of her acceptance that Ben was now sitting with God and the pain was forever gone.

Even Ben's youngest brother felt compelled to honor Ben in his own way: through music. Isaiah wrote "A Letter to My Brother" in a single day in front of a keyboard. Knowing that Isaiah had been having a hard time coping over the past week, I was heartened to see him pull everything together to perform this song at the service. If Isaiah felt nervous or distraught, he sure didn't show it. Isaiah was all smiles in his white coat as he took the stage.

I'd be nervous if I was singing and knew Stevie Wonder was in the audience, but Isaiah looked more comfortable than I'd seen him in a long time. The guitarist was a little out of tune, but that was part of the charm. The pianist began to play some gorgeous notes and chords, and Isaiah started to sing:

This is a letter to you,
To let you know how I feel,
Feeling like this isn't real,
Still wishing you were here with me.
And when I'm sitting alone,
I don't know what to do.
I'm missing you, I'm missing you.

Things running through my head stressing me out.
But I can do it, because you taught me how.
You told me that I don't have to fear no more.
So I won't be afraid.
I won't give up.
I won't let it faze me.
I'll stay tough.

And this is my letter to you. . . .

■ ■ ■

You could feel the power of the Spirit swelling around the church, through all the laughter, hugs, and lovely music coming from the stage. Ben's obituary was read, and we showed a video presentation of Ben that featured highlights of his many media appearances. I loved seeing all the smiles around me. No pity party here.

Stevie Wonder's eulogy was incredibly powerful. I think some people in the church felt a little starstruck with Stevie there, but I always knew him simply as Ben's friend. And Ben thought of Stevie the same way. Since exchanging numbers at the Looking Beyond luncheon, they had kept up an honest friendship that had nothing to do with Grammy awards or fame. Ben hardly knew any of Stevie's music in the first place. They'd simply found a connection as followers of Christ and as men who would never take no for an answer, despite not having sight.

Stevie spoke eloquently of Ben's impact on the world and his undying devotion to God. He encouraged everyone to appreciate the gift of everlasting life that Ben was now enjoying.

The church pianist played in the background as Stevie spoke, letting the notes rise and fall with his words. Stevie said that we were blessed to be witnesses to "the homegoing of a prince of love, who blessed this world with his kindness, with his commitment to God, and with his words of encouragement to those who had sight but not vision—to stand with our own living Emmanuel, as was called Jesus Christ, for he was a God in spirit with us, for the time he lived."

As Stevie finished his remarks a few minutes later, the pianist began to play a little louder. It was time for Stevie to sing. He chose "I Won't Complain" by the late Reverend Paul

Jones, a beautiful song that perfectly sums up Ben's attitude about life and death.

"I want to sing this song," said Stevie, "not out of pain, but out of just understanding that if we are to enjoy each of our lives, sometimes we have challenges. And if we're able to look beyond those and say, 'God, I give you the glory,' then we will be okay, and we will never have to complain."

Stevie had also performed this song at the funerals of his mother, Luther Vandross, and Ray Charles. After all that Ben had endured in the last few years of his life, this song struck a deep chord in my own heart.

Stevie took a deep breath, put the microphone close to his lips, and began to sing in the rich, sweeping voice that's made him a musical legend. I had to nod as he sang about God's response when we ask him why we have so much pain: "He knows what's best for me. . . . So I'll just say, 'Thank you, Lord.' I won't complain."

The band raised the tempo of the song, and we all clapped in rhythm as Stevie sang over and over, "I thank you, Lord; I thank you, Lord!" Soon everyone was on their feet. We were embracing one another, clapping, and shouting praises. The energy in the room was about to go through the roof. I don't think anyone had ever been to a memorial service quite like this.

As Stevie returned from the stage, I prepared to walk up to the front to speak. On my way up, I embraced Stevie, thanking him for those beautiful words and music and for being such a wonderful part of Ben's life.

I know some people might wonder how a mother could

be composed enough to speak at her own teenage son's funeral. But for me, it was a special way to show my love for Ben. I didn't have any kind of prepared speech. I just wanted to speak from the heart and let the Lord guide me.

"Glory be to God!" I shouted while clenching a fist. "Hallelujah! Hallelujah! All I've got to say is God is good, and I thank you, Lord!

"I thank God for Ben's life. He was my little hero. Ben loved God. Before our speaking engagements, we always prayed. He'd say, 'Okay, Momma, don't take all day. You pray too long.' He liked to do his praying on his own.

"Like Stevie said, Ben had real vision: the vision of the hope of true life and life more abundantly. Today would be his seventeenth birthday. And I am celebrating my baby's life because he has abundant life now. He is 100 percent perfectly whole!

"I know a lot of people think I'm supposed to be mourning and shouldn't be able to get out of bed and should be losing my mind. But I know where Ben is. I know that I know. And like Ben said, I just need to be ready to meet him there.

"God bless you all, and thank you so much for coming."

But we weren't done yet. I asked Stevie to come back up. There was one more song that carried a special significance for this day. Ben had died on Martin Luther King Jr. Day. Like I said before, Stevie had released "Happy Birthday" in 1980 in honor of King, as Congress was debating whether to make King's birthday a national holiday. And on this same day of remembrance, we were wishing Ben a happy birthday while celebrating his new life in heaven.

Stevie's "Happy Birthday" is an upbeat song that had everyone clapping along from the second he started playing that piano. Stevie looked so happy while he sang, flashing big smiles between verses. He even changed some of the lyrics to reflect Ben's life, singing, "Today we give celebration to Ben Underwood. . . . Happy birthday to Benjamin Underwood!"

Everybody joined in the singing, with some people literally dancing in the aisles. Hands waved joyously through the church.

"I just want to say it's amazing that we would lose Benjamin on the day that we celebrate the King holiday," said Stevie in between verses. "Praise God!"

By the applause at the end of the song, you would've thought we were at a sold-out concert instead of the funeral of a teenage boy. This was exactly the way to celebrate Ben's new life with the Lord—with joy and music . . . and most of all, with love.

■ ■ ■

Two days after the funeral, Anndrya saw Ben in a dream. It still happens every now and then when she's sleeping.

In her dream, Anndrya saw herself at an elementary school. Suddenly, Ben appeared in front of her.

"Ben, where were you?" she asked.

"I'm right here," said Ben. "I've been here the whole time."

"There were so many people at your funeral. It was amazing!"

"I know. I was right there. That looked like a good time."

"Ben, I still miss you. It's hard for me to not see you."

"'Drya, I'm right here. Don't worry about me."

Ben had always told Anndrya to never be sad about him dying. He'd even get upset when she cried. Anndrya started feeling guilty in the dream, like she'd broken a promise.

"Ben, I really miss you," she said.

"I told you, I'm right here. Just don't cry anymore, okay?"

"I'm trying, Ben, but it's hard."

"If you only knew how good I feel, you wouldn't be sad. Okay, I've got to go."

"You promise me you'll come back?"

"I promise. I'm with you right now, you know. I'll always be here."

Anndrya reached out to hug Ben. Feeling his embrace made her cry. Everything about him felt so real: Ben's warm touch, the sound of his voice, his long braids.

"I love you, Ben."

"I love you, too."

■ ■ ■

Not long after that, Anndrya told me about her dream, as well as the story about the hot sauce packet at Taco Bell. I never have seen Ben in a dream, but I was grateful to hear how this dream had comforted one of his closest friends.

A few months later Anndrya told me she'd been surprised to hear Ben's voice as she was getting ready for prom. Though she and Ben had broken up long before his death, she told me that he'd promised to take her to the dance. He'd passed away a few months before prom, but Anndrya was still planning to go. As she finished dressing and putting on her makeup, she heard Ben's voice. She told me how startled she was. Walking into a nearby room where a TV was on, she realized she was watching Ben in the Channel 5 documentary.

Remembering his promise to take her to the dance, she began to cry.

STILL LEARNING

LOOK AT GOD.

That's what I most want to leave you with. Look at what he did.

He brought Pastor Pugh and Sister Devon into my life at my lowest point as a young mom. And then, after we'd been separated by thousands of miles for many years, he brought us back together just before Ben would begin the fight of his life.

Look at God. Remember how he provided for all my young family's needs when I took a step of faith and moved us to Sacramento.

Look at God. See how he connected my son with Stevie Wonder, giving them both a friend who understood and loved the other.

Look at God. Think how he sent me and Ben off to Japan,

to Hawaii, to Amsterdam—places that fed our souls even as we tried to lift up everyone who saw us.

Look at God. See how Ben's life is still inspiring people and restoring hope. I continue to get messages almost daily through his website, www.benunderwood.com. People who never met Ben—some who'd never even heard of him when he was here—tell me how much his life has touched them.

I could go on and on, pointing to how God showed up in ways that met my deepest needs.

In the years since Ben passed away, life has continued to roll along. I'm still working for the local electric company and attend church every Sunday. I coach and play on a coed softball team and love spending time with my six grandkids.

Tiffany has turned into a responsible young lady. After finishing her degree at Shasta College in Redding, she began working for a petroleum company there.

Joe continues to pursue his dream of rapping and singing professionally. Derius still lives in Sacramento. Isaiah is in Southern California, where he lives with a cousin of mine. He has a job, but I've told him he needs to get on with college soon.

Though I'm a lot more used to it now, the first year after losing Ben was so different and strange. The house was a lot quieter without the phone ringing all the time for Ben and those video game sounds in the front room. It was like a space had been taken from my heart. Sister Devon would sometimes tell me it was okay to slow down, to not fill up my time with so much that I forgot about myself. She told me it was okay to miss Ben.

On the first anniversary of Ben's death, a bunch of his friends came to our house to remember him. It was storming outside, so we gathered in the garage to light candles and share stories about him. One of the local TV stations in Sacramento did a segment to commemorate the anniversary.

It's awesome to see how much Ben still lives in other peoples' hearts. People from all over the world write to say how much my son continues to inspire them. Others remark on how touched they are to see the ways God strengthened our family during Ben's journey. Ben also gets mentioned just about every day on Twitter, and those tweets usually include links to videos of him on YouTube.

Ben has even inspired some people in Hollywood. In a conference call with reporters to promote the movie *The Book of Eli*, Denzel Washington credited Ben as an inspiration behind his character. He'd seen Ben's videos on YouTube and described Ben as "phenomenal."

It just goes to show that Ben continues to fulfill his mission from the Lord, even in death. His purpose was to show people that God is real and that, no matter what their situation is, they can overcome.

■ ■ ■

I want to say something to any parent with a child who is disabled—though I prefer to use the term *different*. And I know I'm speaking to a lot of people. By some estimates, one in every twelve children has some form of disability.

I want you to know that God has blessed you. Not everyone gets to raise children like this, and there's so much to learn from them. I honestly believe these children are like angels, given to parents to teach them how to love unconditionally. How special you are as a man or woman whom God chose to care for that special angel. He promised never to put more on us than we can bear through his strength.

The body of Christ became my refuge in dealing with all of this, and I'm grateful for all the church's support. At the same time, I think most churches can do a lot more for kids like Ben and their families. They can reach out and turn their words and prayers into action. They can visit the sick and their families. They can help them find special services, help them plug into all the public assistance that's out there but that they might not know about, or help them find financial assistance if they need that. (While they're at it, churches can do more with able-bodied kids too. Don't let them sit in the back row and fiddle with their cell phones. Put them down front and challenge them to be great men and women of God. Show them what a blessing good health is, and teach them the importance of Christian kindness toward other kids like Ben, who might not be as outgoing or adaptable as he was.)

We are all made in the image of God, and through our special kids, we all get to understand how beautifully and wonderfully we are made, despite our differences. What is "normal," anyway? Am I normal because I don't have to read braille or because I can hear? The blind and deaf are normal too. They just see and hear in their own way. This insight was powerful for everyone around us, especially Ben's siblings. They learned how to accept other people unconditionally. It was amazing to watch how gentle they were with anybody who was different. That was beautiful.

■ ■ ■

As I reflect on my life, I've come to understand that God equips us with everything we need for whatever we will go through. And I tell you, those storms of life can be heavy. I've dealt with my father and Ben dying, drug addiction, poverty, and watching my child go through major surgeries and chemotherapy. But God gave me the strength to get through it all so I could be here today to share this story. In the midst of all the hardship, I know that God has never left me or forsaken me. I know his Word is alive.

As long as you have hope in the Lord, he'll take you through anything. During my journey, I learned a simple truth: The things I want are not always what the Lord wants. Yet I realize that Ben's cancer was chosen for me. No matter how hard that sounds, I thank God for it because it's taken me to a place in life where I can tell other people with all the conviction in my heart that I know there is hope. In all that we go through, there is hope for every one of us through Christ Jesus.

So why did I title this book *Echoes of an Angel*? I think it reflects what Ben's story is all about. After all, he was able to live like sighted children do because of his clicking and the echoes it made. But far more significant, from an early age he sought to become more spiritually aware and in tune with the Lord's voice. I'm convinced that his lack of sight enabled him to sharpen his spiritual perception. I know he treasured the times he spent alone meditating on God's Word, as well as all the Sundays when he worshiped with fellow believers in church. I suspect that his spiritual sensitivity may also help explain why he sometimes was able to "see" angels, which the Bible describes as "servants—spirits sent to care for people who will inherit salvation" (Hebrews 1:14, NLT). While I never saw these servants of God for myself, I was comforted more than once by this reminder that our Lord never left Ben's side.

Today, the echoes of Ben's life still guide everyone who knew him or learned about him after his death. He's delivering his message to the world loud and clear. In some ways, it's even more powerful now than when he was alive.

When you think about it, nothing else matters but love. We are all divinely and wonderfully made, and I believe that God has given us the choice of which path we want to take in life—anger and bitterness, or love and peace.

I know a couple of parents who've lost their children and now live in anger. We can't gravitate toward resentment. We have to take each life lesson for what it is and make peace with the idea that all situations are chosen for us. Sometimes things get so overwhelming that we have to learn how to hand it all over to the Lord and say "thank you" anyhow.

Sometimes when I'm having a hard day, I remember a friend of Ben's named Jesse, who had lung cancer. Jesse was Ben's age and was very ill by the time he attended Ben's memorial service. After the service ended, I greeted hundreds of people in the foyer. At some point, I saw Jesse's blond head as he slowly made his way up to me.

His very first words to me were, "Guess what? I'm playing football."

I was so excited. "Baby, you play and you be the best out there. Enjoy yourself!"

Here was this kid who was fighting for his life, and yet he was so excited to tell me he was playing football! In fact, Jesse passed away three months later. Yet he lives on in me as a reminder that there will always be someone who needs Ben's story, who needs the hope and peace that only Christ can give.

Sometimes I go to Ben's grave site in Elk Grove. I rub his picture and tell him that I love him. I might shed a few tears, but at the end of the day I am more than okay.

Through Ben, I learned the value of life.

And that what matters most in life is love.

And as the days continue to roll along, I keep in mind that there are no impossibilities in life. It's all in our attitude. It's all in our hope.

ACKNOWLEDGMENTS

AQUANETTA: I want to first give honor to my Lord and Savior Jesus Christ and thank him for blessing me. I want to thank the Tyndale House publishing family and Steve Troha of Folio Literary Management for making this book possible. I also want to thank my writer, Chris Macias, for believing in my story and pushing it to a higher place.

I thank Mrs. Akiyama, Mrs. Barbara, Sister Devon Pugh, Ehan "Goldfingaz" McAlister, and Anndrya for sharing their love and experiences with Ben. I thank Stevie Wonder for his loving spirit and for being there for Ben.

I also want to thank my wonderful family for their support during all my trials and tribulations, especially my aunts: Cynthia, Stephanie, BeBe, and Alice.

CHRIS: I send my deepest thanks and gratitude to: Aquanetta Gordon and family, Rebecca and Floyd Archambeault (and Velvet J.), Kevin Bracy, Tim Swanson, Steve Troha, Sarah Atkinson and the Tyndale House family, the *Sacramento Bee* staff (Joyce Terhaar, Tom Negrete, Janet Vitt, and especially

Cynthia Hubert for first sharing Ben Underwood's story with the wider world), Dahlynn and Ken McKowen, Scott Hervey, Sonny Mayugba, Lore Thaler, Lucy McGinness, Larry and Eleanor Archambeault, Melanie Glover, and Natasha Aguirre. Thank you to my parents, Hope and Jesse Macias; and to my children, Diego and Minka Macias, who inspire every word I write.

DISCUSSION GUIDE

1. Aquanetta's parents and her sometimes difficult childhood led her to resolve that she would always fight for her kids and never let anyone discriminate against them, no matter what. What lessons did you learn from your own upbringing that affect the way you live today? How do you think people can turn their difficult childhood experiences into something positive?

2. The turning point in Aquanetta's battle against addiction was seeing two of her children in foster care and realizing that they might not be returned to her if she didn't change her life. Describe a time when you reached a defining moment in your own battle against a harmful pattern in your life. Why do you think that turning point affected you so much? What did that moment teach you?

3. The Pugh family played a huge role in helping and encouraging Aquanetta and her family. When Aquanetta saw the love Pastor Pugh and Sister Devon

had for her and her children, she began to better understand what it means to be loved by God. What people in your life have demonstrated the love of God for you? What people have been instrumental in your walk with God, especially through tough times?

4. Once Ben was born, Aquanetta focused on trying to reconcile her past mistakes with her hopes for the future. How did this process of reconciliation affect her children and her future? Why do you think this process was so important for her?

5. Ben's cancer diagnosis shook Aquanetta's world. But with God's strength, she faced the challenges before her and her baby, resolving not to ask, *Why me?* but rather, *Why not me?* What do you think it means to ask, *Why not me?* when faced with hardship? How did this perspective help Aquanetta?

6. Even when Ben was about to lose his sight, Aquanetta was determined that her son would thrive and not just survive. What is the difference between the two? Why is it important to do more than just survive?

7. As Ben was growing up, Aquanetta always told him, "Your name is Benjamin Underwood, and you can do anything!" Why do you think Aquanetta chose those words? What is the most encouraging thing a parent, teacher, or other trusted adult told you as you were growing up?

8. As she raised Ben, Aquanetta let him take risks and sometimes do things that seemed dangerous to other parents because she never wanted him to think of

himself as disabled. Why is it so hard to try when you know you might fail? In what areas of your life are you scared of failure?

9. When Ben started at a new school, a lot of his teachers assumed he had limitations and needed to be treated differently from other students. Why do you think Ben's teachers focused on what he couldn't do? Why did Aquanetta want to let Ben do whatever he felt comfortable doing?

10. Once Ben's story became publicized, he and Aquanetta began to receive a lot of media attention. Aquanetta was thankful that she had started going back to church before that happened. Why was it so important for their family to reconnect with a church before their lives began to change? How can a strong church connection be valuable, especially during life transitions?

11. Even though Ben had no eyes, he still had moments of clarity and "vision" that can't be totally explained. What is your reaction to these supernatural stories of sight? Why do you think God gave Ben these experiences?

12. When Ben learned he might have cancer again, he responded by saying that if this was God's will, then it was going to happen. What do you think of Ben's attitude toward his cancer? How would you feel if your child said the same thing?

13. In a moment of frustration, Aquanetta started praying angrily, venting her feelings to God. He reminded her that His will would be done and His strength would

carry her through. Why do you think the idea of God's sovereign plan was encouraging to Aquanetta? Do you find comfort in knowing that God's will is always done?

14. Even after learning he was going to die, Ben never questioned God's purpose. How do you think you would react in that situation? Have you known anyone who exhibited the same kind of peace Ben had?

15. When Ben died, Aquanetta felt sad but also strangely joyful. She missed her son but was happy that he was finally healed and pain-free in heaven. Have you ever experienced conflicting feelings in times of loss? What has helped you reconcile these emotions?

ABOUT THE AUTHORS

AQUANETTA GORDON is the mother of Ben Underwood, who was known around the world as "the boy who could see with sound." Aquanetta and Ben appeared on *The Oprah Winfrey Show*, *The Ellen DeGeneres Show*, *CBS Evening News*, and other TV programs in many different countries. Aquanetta continues to speak about her life with Ben at churches, personal empowerment seminars, and other events. With her son, Aquanetta founded the Ben Underwood Foundation to assist disadvantaged teens. She lives in Sacramento, California.

CHRIS MACIAS is a veteran feature writer for the *Sacramento Bee*. His work includes an award-winning series on south Sacramento's rap scene, and his profile of a former gang member turned pastry chef was included in Da Capo's *Best Food Writing 2012*. Along with interviewing such music legends as Carlos Santana and Al Green, Macias has penned human interest stories that include profiles of young cancer survivors and homeless residents of Sacramento's "Tent City." He holds a BA from the University of California, Davis.

Online Discussion *guide*

TAKE *your* TYNDALE READING
EXPERIENCE *to the* NEXT LEVEL

A FREE discussion guide for this book
is available at bookclubhub.net, perfect
for sparking conversations in your book
group or for digging deeper into the text
on your own.

www.bookclubhub.net

*You'll also find free discussion guides for
other Tyndale books, e-newsletters, e-mail
devotionals, virtual book tours, and more!*

ONE MINUTE
CAN CHANGE YOUR WHOLE LIFE.

"Miracle for Jen will inspire you, challenging your very concept of what it means to know God, as well as to trust Him."

—*JONI EARECKSON TADA*

ISBN 978-1-4143-6120-8

The Barrick family's life was irrevocably changed when a drunk driver careered into their van at eighty miles an hour. The entire family was hurt—but fifteen-year-old Jennifer's injuries were so devastating that paramedics thought she had no chance to live. As Jen lay in a coma, her mother, Linda, pleaded with God to heal Jen from her severe brain trauma—to let her daughter be "normal." When Jen finally awoke, however, it became clear that normal would have to be redefined. She seemed to have gained a new capacity—perhaps a miraculous one—for connecting with God. Discover how God turned normal into extraordinary in this life-changing story of hope and love.

Her tragic accident made headlines.

HER *FAITH* IS CARRYING HER THROUGH.

ISBN 978-1-4143-7670-7

Lauren Scruggs's life and future in the fashion world seemed destined to end the night a spinning plane propeller struck her, causing her to lose her left hand and eye. But God had other plans.

Now Lauren reveals her story in *Still LoLo*: a compelling and fiercely beautiful account of faith, determination, and staying true to who you are—no matter what.

www.StillLoLo.com